© 2024 by FAISAL JAMIL. All rights reserved.

Title: "The Psychology of Consumer Behavior:

Understanding What Drives FMCG Purchases"

This book, along with its contents encompassing text, illustrations, images, diagrams, and other creative elements, is the exclusive property of FAISAL JAMIL and is safeguarded by copyright law.

FAISAL JAMIL asserts full ownership and retains all rights to this book. No part of this publication may be reproduced, distributed, or transmitted in any form or by any means, such as photocopying, recording, or electronic methods, without prior written consent from the copyright holder. Brief quotations in critical reviews and certain noncommercial uses permitted by copyright law are exceptions.

This copyright notice applies to all editions, formats, and translations of the book, whether in print, digital, or any other medium or technology existing now or developed in the future. Unauthorized use or infringement may result in legal action and pursuit of remedies under applicable copyright laws.

While efforts have been made to ensure accuracy and reliability, FAISAL JAMIL does not guarantee the completeness or suitability of the information. Readers are responsible for evaluating and using the content judiciously.

FAISAL JAMIL reserves the right to make changes, updates, or corrections to the book without prior notice. Inclusion of third-party materials or references does not imply endorsement or affiliation unless used under fair use principles or with proper permissions and attributions.

For permissions, inquiries, or requests regarding the book's use, please contact FAISAL JAMIL through official channels listed on their Amazon author page or provided email address.

This comprehensive copyright notice serves to protect FAISAL JAMIL'S intellectual property rights, maintain content control, and inform users about associated restrictions and permissions.

Warm regards,

FAISAL JAMIL

I Always Give's Free Copies Need Your Feedback And

Reviews Keeps In Touch!

http://www.amazon.com/author/faisal.jamil

Email: faisaljamilauthor@gmail.com

About the author

Certainly! Faisal Jamil is a multifaceted individual with a diverse set of skills and experiences. With a strong foundation in computer knowledge since childhood, he has developed a deep understanding of technology that informs his work as a content writer. Faisal also possesses digital skills, which further enhance his abilities in various digital platforms and technologies.

Beyond his professional endeavors, Faisal Jamil has also excelled in the martial arts, particularly Shotokan Karate, where he achieved the prestigious rank of first Dan black belt. This achievement speaks to his dedication, discipline, and commitment to personal growth and mastery.

In his professional life, Faisal Jamil has carved out a successful career in sales management within the Fast Moving Consumer Goods (FMCG) sector. His roles in various FMCG companies have honed his skills in strategic planning, team leadership, and business development. Faisal's ability to drive sales and achieve targets has been instrumental in his career progression, showcasing his talent for identifying opportunities and delivering results.

Faisal Jamil is also deeply interested in business investment strategies, planning, and execution. His understanding of these areas has been key to his success in the business world, allowing him to make informed decisions and implement effective strategies. His ability to navigate the complexities of investment planning and execution has set him apart as a strategic thinker and a valuable asset in any business endeavor.

Overall, Faisal Jamil is a dynamic individual who combines his passion for technology, martial arts, sales management, digital skills, and business investment strategies to achieve success in diverse fields. His journey is a testament to his versatility, resilience, and continuous pursuit of excellence.

Yours Sincerely

FAISAL JAMIL

I Always Give's Free Copies Need Your Feedback And

Reviews Keeps In Touch!

https://www.amazon.com/author/faisal.jamil

Email: faisaljamilauthor@gmail.com

THE PSYCHOLOGY OF
CONSUMER BEHAVIOR
UNDERSTANDING WHAT DRIVES
FMCG PURCHASES

Table of Content

Preface --11

Introduction ---14

Chapter 1: Introduction to Consumer Behavior -----------20

Understanding consumer behavior in FMCG

Importance of studying consumer psychology

Chapter 2: Consumer Decision-Making Process -----------25

Need recognition and problem awareness

Information search and evaluation

Chapter 3: Psychological Factors Influencing Consumer Behavior ---31

Motivation and needs

Perception and sensation

Chapter 4: Social and Cultural Influences ------------------37

Family, reference groups, and social classes

Culture and subculture influences

Chapter 5: Attitudes and Attitude Change ------------------43

Formation of attitudes

Changing consumer attitudes

Chapter 6: Personality and Consumer Behavior -----------49

The role of personality traits

Brand personality and consumer preference

Chapter 7: Lifestyle and Consumer Behavior ---------------55

Understanding consumer lifestyles

Lifestyle segmentation in FMCG

Chapter 8: Consumer Perception of Product Quality ----61

Factors influencing perceived quality

Implications for FMCG marketing

Chapter 9: Brand Loyalty and Brand Equity ----------------68

Building brand loyalty in FMCG

Measuring brand equity

Chapter 10: Pricing and Consumer Behavior ---------------75

Price perception and sensitivity

Psychological pricing strategies

Chapter 11: Promotions and Consumer Behavior --------82

Impact of promotions on consumer decisions

Promotional strategies in FMCG

Chapter 12: Packaging and Visual Appeal -------------------90

Importance of packaging in FMCG

Psychological aspects of packaging design

Chapter 13: Consumer Decision Heuristics ------------------97

Types of decision-making shortcuts

Impulse buying behavior

Chapter 14: Cross-Cultural Consumer Behavior ---------104

Cultural differences in FMCG consumption

Adapting marketing strategies globally

Chapter 15: Consumer Emotions and Purchasing Decisions ---111

Emotional triggers in FMCG marketing

Emotional branding strategies

Chapter 16: The Role of Advertising ------------------------118

Psychological principles in advertising

Effective advertising strategies in FMCG

Chapter 17: Consumer Behavior in Digital Age ------------125

Online shopping behavior

Influence of digital marketing on FMCG purchases

Chapter 18: Consumer Satisfaction and Post-Purchase Behavior --133

Factors influencing satisfaction

Post-purchase dissonance and loyalty

Chapter 19: Ethical Considerations in Consumer Behavior --------139

Ethical consumerism trends

Corporate social responsibility in FMCG

Chapter 20: Innovation and Consumer Adoption -------146

Adopting new products in FMCG

Innovation strategies and consumer psychology

Chapter 21: Environmental and Sustainability Issues --153

Green consumerism trends

Sustainable practices in FMCG

Chapter 22: Psychological Aspects of Brand Switching --------160

Reasons for brand switching

Retaining customers in competitive markets

Chapter 23: Consumer Behavior Research Methods ---167

Qualitative and quantitative approaches

Case studies in FMCG consumer research

Chapter 24: Future Trends in Consumer Behavior ------175

Predicting consumer behavior shifts

Emerging trends in FMCG marketing

Chapter 25: Conclusion --182

Summarizing key insights

Implications for FMCG marketers

Preface

In the dynamic and highly competitive world of fast-moving consumer goods (FMCG), understanding what drives consumer behavior is more crucial than ever. Every day, consumers make countless decisions about what products to buy, influenced by a complex interplay of psychological, social, and cultural factors. This book, "The Psychology of Consumer Behavior: Understanding What Drives FMCG Purchases," aims to unravel these complexities and provide valuable insights into the minds of consumers.

The inspiration for this book comes from the rapid evolution of the FMCG industry, where trends shift swiftly, and consumer preferences are in constant flux. As technology advances and markets globalize, the need for a deeper understanding of consumer behavior has become paramount. This book seeks to bridge the gap between theoretical knowledge and practical application, offering both academic insights and actionable strategies for marketers and business professionals.

Throughout my career in marketing and consumer research, I have witnessed firsthand the profound impact that a nuanced understanding of consumer behavior can have on a company's success. Whether it's through the design of a product, the development of a marketing campaign, or the creation of a brand identity, the ability to tap into consumer psychology can make the difference between a product that flies off the shelves and one that gathers dust.

This book is structured to provide a comprehensive overview of the key elements influencing consumer behavior in the FMCG sector. We start with the fundamentals of consumer decision-making processes, exploring how consumers recognize needs, search for information, and evaluate their options. From there, we delve into the psychological underpinnings of consumer behavior, including motivation, perception, and the formation of attitudes.

We also examine the powerful role of social and cultural influences, such as family, reference groups, and cultural norms, in shaping consumer preferences. In addition, the book covers critical topics like brand loyalty, pricing strategies, the impact of promotions, and the importance of packaging design. Each chapter is designed to provide both theoretical insights and practical examples, ensuring that readers can apply the concepts to real-world scenarios.

In the digital age, consumer behavior is continually evolving, and this book addresses the latest trends and challenges, including the rise of online shopping, the influence of digital marketing, and the growing importance of sustainability and ethical considerations. By understanding these emerging trends, marketers can better anticipate and respond to the changing needs and expectations of their consumers.

"The Psychology of Consumer Behavior: Understanding What Drives FMCG Purchases" is intended for a broad audience, including marketing professionals, business students, and anyone interested in the intricate workings of consumer psychology. My hope is that this book will serve as a valuable resource, providing readers with the knowledge and tools they need to navigate the ever-changing landscape of the FMCG industry successfully.

As we embark on this journey into the mind of the consumer, I encourage you to think critically about the concepts presented and consider how they can be applied to your own experiences and challenges. By gaining a deeper understanding of what drives consumer behavior, we can create more meaningful connections with our customers, foster brand loyalty, and ultimately drive business success.

Thank you for joining me on this exploration of consumer psychology. I hope you find this book both informative and inspiring.

Sincerely,

FAISAL JAMIL

INTRODUCTION

In the realm of fast-moving consumer goods (FMCG), where the market is saturated with a multitude of products competing for consumer attention, understanding the psychology behind consumer behavior is more important than ever. Every purchase decision, whether it's choosing a brand of toothpaste or a type of snack, is influenced by a complex web of factors that marketers and businesses must decipher to stay ahead. This book, "The Psychology of Consumer Behavior: Understanding What Drives FMCG Purchases," is designed to unravel these complexities and provide actionable insights into the minds of consumers.

The FMCG sector is characterized by high volume, low margin sales, and a rapid turnover of products. Unlike durable goods, FMCG items such as food, beverages, toiletries, and cleaning products are purchased frequently and consumed quickly. The speed and frequency of these purchases make it essential for businesses to have a deep understanding of what drives consumer choices.

At the heart of consumer behavior lies the decision-making process. Consumers go through various stages from need recognition, information search, and evaluation of alternatives, to the actual purchase decision and post-purchase behavior. Each stage is influenced by a myriad of factors, including psychological, social, and cultural elements. This book delves into these stages, providing a detailed examination of how each factor impacts consumer decisions.

Psychological factors such as motivation, perception, and attitude formation play a crucial role in shaping consumer behavior. Understanding what motivates consumers, how they perceive products and brands, and how their attitudes are formed and changed can provide invaluable insights for marketers. This book explores these psychological aspects in depth, offering strategies to influence consumer behavior effectively.

Social and cultural influences are equally significant. Family, friends, social classes, and cultural norms all contribute to shaping consumer preferences and behaviors. In a globalized world, cultural differences become particularly important, as they can drastically alter how consumers perceive and interact with products. This book examines these social and cultural dimensions, providing strategies for adapting marketing efforts to different contexts.

In today's digital age, consumer behavior is rapidly evolving. The rise of e-commerce, social media, and digital marketing has transformed how consumers interact with brands and make purchasing decisions. This book addresses these changes, exploring the impact of digital technologies on consumer behavior and offering insights into how businesses can leverage these tools to connect with consumers more effectively.

One of the most significant trends in consumer behavior is the growing emphasis on sustainability and ethical consumption. Modern consumers are increasingly concerned with the environmental and social impact of their purchases. This book explores the implications of this trend for the FMCG sector, highlighting the importance of sustainable practices and ethical marketing.

Innovation is another key theme in the FMCG industry. With consumers constantly seeking new and improved products, businesses must continuously innovate to stay relevant.

This book examines the psychological factors that drive innovation adoption and provides strategies for successfully introducing new products to the market.

Throughout this book, we will also explore various research methods used to study consumer behavior. From qualitative approaches like focus groups and interviews to quantitative techniques such as surveys and experiments, understanding these methods will enable businesses to gather and interpret valuable consumer insights.

"The Psychology of Consumer Behavior: Understanding What Drives FMCG Purchases" aims to equip readers with a comprehensive understanding of the factors influencing consumer behavior and practical strategies for applying this knowledge. Whether you are a marketing professional, a business student, or simply interested in the intricacies of consumer psychology, this book will provide you with the tools you need to navigate the complex world of FMCG marketing.

As we embark on this journey into the mind of the consumer, we invite you to think critically about the concepts presented and consider how they can be applied to your own experiences and challenges. By gaining a deeper understanding of what drives consumer behavior, we can create more meaningful connections with our customers, foster brand loyalty, and ultimately drive business success.

Welcome to "The Psychology of Consumer Behavior: Understanding What Drives FMCG Purchases." Let's delve into the fascinating world of consumer psychology and uncover the secrets behind successful FMCG marketing.

Chapter 1
Introduction to Consumer Behavior

Understanding Consumer Behavior in FMCG

Consumer behavior is the study of how individuals, groups, and organizations make decisions regarding the selection, purchase, use, and disposal of goods, services, ideas, or experiences to satisfy their needs and desires. In the context of Fast Moving Consumer Goods (FMCG), this understanding is particularly crucial for several reasons:

1: High Purchase Frequency: FMCG products, which include everyday items such as food, beverages, personal care products, and household items, are characterized by their high purchase frequency. This means consumers buy these items regularly, often weekly or monthly. Due to this high turnover rate, even minor shifts in consumer behavior can significantly impact sales and market share. Companies need to understand these behaviors to predict demand accurately and manage inventory efficiently.

2: Low Involvement Purchases: FMCG products are typically low involvement purchases, meaning consumers spend less time and effort on decision-making compared to high involvement products like cars or electronics. However, despite the lower effort, psychological factors like brand recognition, packaging, and promotional offers still play a significant role in influencing purchase decisions. Understanding these nuances can help companies design more effective

3: Brand Loyalty and Switching: Building and maintaining brand loyalty is a critical objective for FMCG companies. Consumers often exhibit habitual purchasing behaviors, sticking to brands they trust. Understanding the drivers of brand loyalty, such as perceived quality, emotional connection, and past experiences, can help companies retain customers. Conversely, understanding why consumers switch brands, such as dissatisfaction, better alternatives, or promotional offers, can help in developing strategies to attract new customers.

4: Competitive Market Dynamics: The FMCG sector is highly competitive, with numerous brands vying for consumer attention and market share. To stand out in this crowded market, companies need to understand consumer preferences and behaviors deeply. This knowledge helps in differentiating their products, creating compelling value propositions, and positioning their brands effectively.

5: Dynamic Consumer Preferences: Consumer preferences in the FMCG sector can change rapidly due to various factors, including trends, innovations, economic conditions, and cultural shifts. For example, the growing awareness of health and wellness has driven demand for organic and natural products. Continuous study of consumer behavior allows companies to stay ahead of these changes, adapt their strategies accordingly, and capitalize on emerging opportunities.

Importance of Studying Consumer Psychology

Consumer psychology is a specialized branch of psychology that focuses on understanding the underlying psychological mechanisms that drive consumer behaviors. It examines the motivations, attitudes, perceptions, and decision-making processes of consumers. In the FMCG sector, the study of consumer psychology is particularly important for several reasons:

1: Influencing Purchase Decisions: By understanding the psychological factors that influence purchase decisions, companies can design marketing strategies that effectively appeal to their target audience. For instance, advertisements that evoke positive emotions or highlight the benefits of a product can significantly impact consumer choices. Additionally, understanding the role of heuristics and biases in decision-making can help in crafting persuasive messages and offers.

2: Product Development and Innovation: Insights from consumer psychology can guide the development of new products that meet consumer needs and preferences. For example, understanding that consumers seek convenience can lead to the creation of easy-to-use packaging or ready-to-eat food products. By aligning product features with consumer desires, companies can increase the likelihood of new product success.

3: Enhancing Customer Experience: Applying psychological principles can enhance the overall customer experience. This includes aspects such as packaging design, in-store displays, online shopping interfaces, and customer service interactions. For example, using colors and designs that attract attention or creating a seamless and enjoyable shopping experience can positively influence consumer perceptions and behaviors.

4: Effective Communication: Understanding how consumers process information is crucial for crafting effective communication strategies. This involves choosing the right communication channels, crafting messages that resonate with the target audience, and using visuals that capture attention. For instance, knowing that consumers are more likely to remember visual information can guide the creation of impactful advertisements and packaging.

5: Behavioral Segmentation: Segmenting the market based on consumer behavior allows for more targeted and efficient marketing. Traditional demographic segmentation may not fully capture the diversity of consumer behaviors and preferences. Behavioral segmentation, which considers factors such as purchase frequency, brand loyalty, and shopping habits, enables companies to tailor their marketing efforts to specific consumer segments, resulting in more effective and personalized marketing campaigns.

6: Building Brand Identity and Equity: A strong brand identity that resonates with consumers' self-image and aspirations can foster loyalty and advocacy. Understanding the psychological connections consumers make with brands helps in building and maintaining a strong brand identity. For example, brands that align with consumers' values and lifestyles, such as sustainability or health-consciousness, can create a deeper emotional connection and build brand equity.

Conclusion

In conclusion, understanding consumer behavior and psychology is fundamental for success in the FMCG sector. It enables companies to create products and marketing strategies that resonate with consumers, build strong brand loyalty, and stay competitive in a dynamic market. As consumer preferences continue to evolve, ongoing research and adaptation are essential for maintaining a deep connection with consumers and driving business growth. By leveraging insights from consumer behavior and psychology, FMCG companies can develop strategies that not only meet the current needs of consumers but also anticipate and shape future trends, ensuring long-term success in the market.

Chapter 2
Consumer Decision-Making Process

Understanding the consumer decision-making process is crucial for marketers in the FMCG sector. This process involves several stages through which a consumer moves from recognizing a need to making a purchase and evaluating the outcome. By comprehensively understanding these stages, companies can design strategies that effectively influence consumer decisions at each step. This chapter focuses on two critical stages: need recognition and problem awareness, and information search and evaluation.

Need Recognition and Problem Awareness

The consumer decision-making process begins with the recognition of a need or problem. This stage is fundamental because it triggers the entire buying process. Here's a deeper look into how need recognition and problem awareness occur:

1: Internal and External Stimuli: Need recognition can be prompted by internal stimuli (such as hunger, thirst, or boredom) or external stimuli (such as marketing messages, social influences, or environmental factors). For example, seeing an advertisement for a new snack can make a consumer realize they are hungry or curious about trying something new.

2: Types of Needs:

Functional Needs: These are practical needs related to the basic function or utility of a product. For example, a consumer may recognize the need for toothpaste to maintain dental hygiene.

Emotional Needs: These needs are tied to feelings, emotions, and psychological satisfaction. For example, buying a specific brand of coffee because it makes the consumer feel sophisticated or because it evokes pleasant memories.

Social Needs: These are related to the consumer's desire to fit in or be accepted by a group. For instance, purchasing a particular brand of clothing to be perceived as trendy or fashionable.

3: Need Recognition in FMCG: In the FMCG sector, need recognition often involves habitual and low-involvement products. Consumers might not spend much time deliberating over their need for these products but will respond quickly to stimuli. Effective marketing strategies can help trigger need recognition through various channels, such as advertisements, in-store displays, and social media promotions.

4: Problem Awareness: This is closely related to need recognition and involves the consumer becoming aware of a problem that needs solving. For instance, realizing they are running out of laundry detergent and need to buy more. Problem awareness can be heightened by situations like promotions (e.g., "limited-time offer") or new product launches that highlight a gap or need in the consumer's current product usage.

Information Search and Evaluation

Once a need or problem is recognized, consumers move to the information search and evaluation stage. This stage involves gathering information about potential solutions and evaluating the available options. Here's a detailed exploration of this stage:

1: Information Search:

Internal Search: This involves recalling information from memory based on past experiences, knowledge, and perceptions. For example, remembering a particular brand of shampoo that worked well in the past.

External Search: This involves seeking information from external sources, such as friends, family, advertisements, online reviews, and retail displays. The extent of external search depends on factors like the importance of the purchase, the perceived risk, and the consumer's prior knowledge.

2: Sources of Information:

Personal Sources: Family, friends, and acquaintances who provide recommendations and reviews based on their experiences.

Commercial Sources: Advertisements, salespeople, packaging, and displays that provide product information and persuasive messages.

Public Sources: Online reviews, consumer reports, and social media where unbiased information and opinions are shared.

Experiential Sources: Direct experiences, such as product trials, samples, or demonstrations.

3: Factors Influencing Information Search:

Perceived Risk: Higher perceived risk (financial, social, or psychological) leads to more extensive information search.

Consumer Involvement: Higher involvement in the product category results in more active and detailed information search.

Market Characteristics: The availability of information, the number of alternatives, and the complexity of the product category influence the extent of the information search.

4: Evaluation of Alternatives:

Criteria for Evaluation: Consumers use various criteria to evaluate alternatives, such as price, quality, brand reputation, and specific product features. For FMCG products, convenience, taste, packaging, and perceived health benefits are common criteria.

Decision Rules: Consumers apply decision rules to simplify the evaluation process. These rules can be compensatory (weighing all attributes and making trade-offs) or non-compensatory (rejecting options that don't meet certain criteria).

5: Evaluation in FMCG:

Brand Loyalty: For habitual purchases, brand loyalty can simplify the evaluation process as consumers repeatedly choose the same brand without extensive evaluation.

Promotions and Discounts: Special offers, discounts, and promotions can significantly influence the evaluation process by providing additional value to consumers.

Packaging and Labels: In FMCG, packaging and labels play a crucial role in the evaluation process. Attractive packaging and clear, informative labels can sway consumer decisions.

Conclusion

The stages of need recognition and problem awareness, followed by information search and evaluation, are critical components of the consumer decision-making process. In the FMCG sector, understanding these stages allows companies to design marketing strategies that effectively trigger needs, provide relevant information, and influence the evaluation of alternatives. By tapping into the psychological and behavioral aspects of consumers, FMCG marketers can create compelling propositions that resonate with their target audience and drive purchase decisions. This understanding ultimately leads to better product positioning, increased customer satisfaction, and stronger brand loyalty.

Chapter 3
Psychological Factors Influencing Consumer Behavior

Understanding the psychological factors that influence consumer behavior is crucial for effectively marketing FMCG products. These factors help explain why consumers make certain purchasing decisions and how they interact with brands and products. In this chapter, we will explore two key psychological factors: motivation and needs, and perception and sensation.

Motivation and Needs

Motivation refers to the internal driving forces that compel consumers to take action to satisfy their needs and desires. Needs are the basic requirements and desires that consumers seek to fulfill. Together, these concepts form the foundation of consumer behavior.

1: Maslow's Hierarchy of Needs: This theory, proposed by Abraham Maslow, categorizes human needs into a hierarchical structure, with basic needs at the bottom and higher-level needs at the top. The hierarchy includes:

Physiological Needs: Basic survival needs such as food, water, and shelter. In the context of FMCG, products like groceries and bottled water fulfill these needs.

Safety Needs: The need for security and protection. FMCG products such as cleaning supplies and hygiene products cater to safety needs.

Social Needs: The need for love, belonging, and social interaction. Products like snacks and beverages consumed in social settings can fulfill these needs.

Esteem Needs: The need for respect, self-esteem, and recognition. Premium brands and luxury FMCG items can satisfy esteem needs.

Self-Actualization Needs: The need for personal growth and self-fulfillment. Products that promote a healthy lifestyle or environmental sustainability can address these needs.

2: Types of Motivation:

Intrinsic Motivation: Driven by internal rewards and personal satisfaction. For example, a consumer might buy organic food because it aligns with their health and ethical values.

Extrinsic Motivation: Driven by external rewards and incentives. Promotional offers, discounts, and loyalty programs are examples of extrinsic motivators in FMCG.

3: The Role of Motivation in FMCG:

Impulsive Purchases: Motivations can drive impulsive buying behavior, where consumers make spontaneous purchases without extensive planning. This is common in FMCG, where products are often displayed near checkout counters to trigger impulsive decisions.

Brand Loyalty: Motivation plays a key role in building and maintaining brand loyalty. Consumers motivated by positive past experiences, perceived quality, and emotional connections are more likely to remain loyal to a brand.

Health and Wellness Trends: Increasing consumer motivation towards health and wellness has driven the demand for organic, natural, and low-calorie FMCG products. Companies that understand and tap into these motivations can better meet consumer needs.

Perception and Sensation

Perception and sensation are critical psychological factors that influence how consumers interpret and respond to marketing stimuli. Sensation involves the immediate response of sensory receptors (sight, sound, touch, taste, and smell) to stimuli, while perception is the process by which individuals select, organize, and interpret these sensations.

1: Sensation:

Visual Sensation: The most dominant sense in consumer behavior. Factors such as color, design, and visual appeal of packaging can significantly impact consumer decisions. For example, bright colors can attract attention, while clean and minimalist designs can convey quality and sophistication.

Auditory Sensation: Sound can influence consumer behavior through advertising jingles, in-store music, and product sounds (e.g., the crunch of a snack).

Olfactory Sensation: Smell plays a powerful role in consumer behavior, especially for food and personal care products. Pleasant scents can evoke positive emotions and memories, influencing purchase decisions.

Tactile Sensation: The feel of a product or its packaging can impact consumer perception of quality. For example, a well-designed, sturdy packaging can convey a sense of premium quality.

Gustatory Sensation: Taste is crucial for food and beverage products. Sampling and tastings can be effective marketing strategies to influence consumer preferences and drive purchases.

2: Perception:

Selective Attention: Consumers are exposed to a vast amount of information daily, but they only pay attention to a small portion of it. Marketers must create compelling and attention-grabbing content to capture consumer attention.

Selective Distortion: Consumers interpret information in a way that fits their preconceptions and beliefs. For instance, loyal customers may perceive their favorite brand more positively, even if the objective quality is the same as competitors.

Selective Retention: Consumers remember information that supports their beliefs and forget information that contradicts them. Effective marketing strategies ensure that key messages are memorable and align with consumer values.

3: Influencing Consumer Perception in FMCG:

Brand Image and Positioning: A strong brand image can positively influence consumer perception. Consistent messaging, high-quality products, and positive associations (e.g., trustworthiness, sustainability) can enhance brand perception.

Packaging Design: Packaging plays a crucial role in shaping consumer perception. Innovative, functional, and aesthetically pleasing packaging can attract consumers and differentiate products from competitors.

Advertising and Promotion: Effective advertising leverages visual and auditory cues to create positive associations and influence consumer perception. Promotions, such as discounts and special offers, can also impact perceived value and urgency.

Conclusion

Motivation and needs, along with perception and sensation, are fundamental psychological factors that drive consumer behavior. Understanding these factors allows FMCG marketers to design strategies that resonate with consumers, address their needs and motivations, and influence their perceptions and decisions. By leveraging insights from psychology, companies can create compelling products and marketing campaigns that connect with consumers on a deeper level, ultimately driving brand loyalty and business success.

Chapter 4
Social and Cultural Influences

In the realm of consumer behavior, social and cultural influences play a significant role in shaping how individuals perceive, evaluate, and purchase products. Understanding these influences is crucial for FMCG marketers as they develop strategies to connect with their target audience. This chapter explores the impact of family, reference groups, social classes, culture, and subcultures on consumer behavior.

Family, Reference Groups, and Social Classes

1: Family Influence:

Roles and Decision-Making: The family unit is a primary source of influence on consumer behavior. Family members often play different roles in the decision-making process, such as initiators, influencers, deciders, buyers, and users. For example, parents might decide on the brand of cereal to buy, influenced by children's preferences.

Life Cycle Stages: Different stages of the family life cycle, such as young singles, married couples, families with children, and empty nesters, have distinct consumption patterns and preferences. Marketers need to tailor their strategies to address the specific needs and behaviors of each stage.

Intergenerational Influence: Consumer preferences and brand loyalties can be passed down from one generation to the next. For instance, a family's tradition of using a particular brand of ketchup can influence younger members to adopt the same brand.

2: Reference Groups:

Definition and Types: Reference groups are groups of people that individuals use as a standard for evaluating their own behavior. These can include friends, colleagues, celebrities, and even online communities. There are several types of reference groups:

Primary Groups: Groups with which individuals have regular, direct interaction, such as family and close friends.

Secondary Groups: Larger, more formal groups with less frequent interaction, such as professional associations or clubs.

Aspirational Groups: Groups to which individuals aspire to belong, often influencing them to purchase products that align with the group's norms and values.

Dissociative Groups: Groups that individuals do not wish to associate with, influencing them to avoid certain products or brands.

Influence Mechanisms: Reference groups influence consumer behavior through various mechanisms, including:

Normative Influence: When individuals conform to the expectations of a group to gain approval or avoid disapproval.

Informational Influence: When individuals seek information from a group to make informed decisions.

Value-Expressive Influence: When individuals adopt behaviors or products to express values or identity that align with the group.

3: Social Classes:

Definition and Characteristics: Social class refers to the hierarchical divisions in society based on factors such as income, education, occupation, and lifestyle. Social classes are typically categorized into lower, middle, and upper classes.

Impact on Consumer Behavior: Social class influences consumption patterns, preferences, and brand perceptions. For instance:

Lower Class: Consumers in this group may prioritize affordability and value, often opting for store brands or discount products.

Middle Class: This group may seek a balance between quality and price, favoring brands that offer perceived value and reliability.

Upper Class: Consumers in this group may prioritize luxury, exclusivity, and premium quality, often opting for high-end brands and products.

Aspirational Behavior: Individuals often aspire to move up the social ladder and may purchase products associated with higher social classes to signal their desired status.

Culture and Subculture Influences

1: Culture:

Definition and Components: Culture is the set of shared values, beliefs, norms, and customs that shape the behavior of a group of people. It encompasses language, religion, traditions, and social behaviors.

Cultural Dimensions:

Individualism vs. Collectivism: Individualistic cultures emphasize personal goals and achievements, while collectivist cultures prioritize group harmony and collective goals.

Power Distance: The extent to which less powerful members of society accept and expect power to be distributed unequally. High power distance cultures may show deference to authority and brand status.

Uncertainty Avoidance: The degree to which a culture tolerates ambiguity and uncertainty. Cultures with high uncertainty avoidance prefer clear rules and structure, influencing their trust in established brands.

Masculinity vs. Femininity: Masculine cultures value competitiveness and achievement, while feminine cultures value care and quality of life.

Impact on Consumer Behavior: Cultural values shape consumer preferences and behaviors. For example, in individualistic cultures, consumers may prefer products that emphasize personal benefits and uniqueness, while in collectivist cultures, products that promote group harmony and family values may be favored.

2: Subculture:

Definition and Characteristics: Subcultures are distinct cultural groups within a larger culture that share unique values, norms, and behaviors. Subcultures can be based on factors such as ethnicity, religion, geographic region, and lifestyle.

Ethnic Subcultures: Different ethnic groups may have unique consumption patterns and preferences. For example, Hispanic consumers in the U.S. may favor brands that celebrate their cultural heritage and offer products tailored to their tastes.

Religious Subcultures: Religious beliefs and practices can influence consumer behavior, such as dietary restrictions, holiday-related purchases, and preferences for products that align with religious values.

Geographic Subcultures: Regional differences can lead to variations in consumer behavior. For instance, consumers in urban areas may prefer convenience-oriented products, while those in rural areas may prioritize practicality and durability.

Lifestyle Subcultures: Groups with shared interests and lifestyles, such as health enthusiasts, environmentalists, or technology geeks, exhibit distinct consumption patterns. For example, health-conscious consumers may prioritize organic and natural products, while tech enthusiasts may seek the latest gadgets and innovations.

Conclusion

Social and cultural influences are powerful determinants of consumer behavior. Family dynamics, reference groups, social class, culture, and subculture all shape how consumers perceive, evaluate, and purchase FMCG products. By understanding these influences, marketers can develop strategies that resonate with consumers on a deeper level, creating more effective and targeted marketing campaigns. This understanding allows companies to build stronger connections with their target audience, ultimately driving brand loyalty and long-term success in the competitive FMCG market.

Chapter 5
Attitudes and Attitude Change

Attitudes play a crucial role in influencing consumer behavior. They shape how consumers perceive products and brands, their purchase intentions, and their loyalty. Understanding how attitudes are formed and how they can be changed is essential for FMCG marketers aiming to influence consumer decisions effectively.

Formation of Attitudes

An attitude is a learned predisposition to respond in a consistently favorable or unfavorable manner with respect to a given object, such as a product, brand, service, or idea. Attitudes are formed through a combination of cognitive, affective, and behavioral components:

1: Cognitive Component:

Beliefs and Knowledge: The cognitive component consists of the beliefs and knowledge a consumer has about a product or brand. These beliefs are formed based on direct experience, information from advertisements, word-of-mouth, and other sources. For example, a consumer might believe that a particular brand of toothpaste is effective in preventing cavities because of information obtained from advertisements or recommendations from a dentist.

Attributes and Benefits: Consumers form attitudes based on the attributes of a product (e.g., taste, packaging, price) and the benefits they perceive from using it (e.g., health benefits, convenience).

2: Affective Component:

Emotions and Feelings: The affective component involves the emotions and feelings associated with a product or brand. These emotional responses can be positive, negative, or neutral. For example, a consumer might feel a sense of nostalgia when seeing a brand of candy they enjoyed as a child, leading to a positive attitude toward the brand.

Emotional Appeals in Advertising: Marketers often use emotional appeals in advertising to create positive associations with their products. This can include using heartwarming stories, humor, or aspirational imagery to elicit positive emotions.

3: Behavioral Component:

Actions and Intentions: The behavioral component reflects the consumer's intended or actual behavior toward the product or brand. This includes purchase intentions, usage behavior, and loyalty. For example, a consumer who has a positive attitude toward a brand of laundry detergent is more likely to purchase it regularly and recommend it to others.

Changing Consumer Attitudes

Changing consumer attitudes can be a challenging but essential task for marketers, especially when launching new products, repositioning existing brands, or responding to negative perceptions. There are several strategies to change consumer attitudes effectively:

1: Persuasion Techniques:

Message Framing: Presenting information in a way that emphasizes the positive aspects of a product or minimizes the negatives can influence attitudes. For instance, highlighting the health benefits of a snack rather than focusing on its low-calorie content.

Two-Sided Messages: Addressing both the pros and cons of a product can enhance credibility and trust. This approach works well when consumers are skeptical or well-informed. For example, an ad for a new toothpaste might acknowledge that it is slightly more expensive but emphasize its superior cavity-fighting properties.

2: Source Credibility and Attractiveness:

Expert Endorsements: Using experts or credible figures to endorse a product can enhance the perceived trustworthiness and effectiveness of the product. For example, a skincare brand might use dermatologists to endorse their products.

Celebrity Endorsements: Celebrities can attract attention and create positive associations with a brand, especially if they are well-liked and relevant to the target audience. However, the credibility of the endorsement depends on the fit between the celebrity and the product.

3: Classical Conditioning:

Association with Positive Stimuli: Classical conditioning involves associating a product with positive stimuli to elicit a favorable response. For example, using pleasant music, attractive visuals, or heartwarming scenes in advertisements can create positive associations with the product.

Repetition and Consistency: Repeated exposure to the product paired with positive stimuli reinforces the association and strengthens the attitude. Consistent messaging across various marketing channels also helps in reinforcing the desired attitude.

4: Cognitive Dissonance Reduction:

Post-Purchase Reinforcement: After a purchase, consumers may experience cognitive dissonance, where their beliefs about the product are challenged by their experiences. Marketers can reduce dissonance by providing reassurance through follow-up communications, satisfaction guarantees, and positive reinforcement. For example, sending a thank-you email with tips on how to use the product effectively.

Aligning Marketing Messages with Consumer Beliefs: Ensuring that marketing messages align with the existing beliefs and values of the target audience can minimize dissonance and facilitate attitude change. For instance, promoting the eco-friendly aspects of a product to environmentally conscious consumers.

5: Behavioral Influence:

Trial and Sampling: Encouraging consumers to try a product can lead to attitude change through direct experience. Free samples, trial offers, and demonstrations allow consumers to experience the benefits firsthand, leading to more favorable attitudes.

Incentives and Promotions: Offering incentives, such as discounts, coupons, or loyalty rewards, can motivate consumers to try a product or switch brands. Positive experiences during the trial period can lead to long-term attitude change.

6: Social Influence:

Opinion Leaders and Influencers: Leveraging opinion leaders and social media influencers who have credibility and reach within the target audience can effectively change attitudes. These individuals can provide authentic reviews and recommendations that resonate with their followers.

Social Proof: Demonstrating that a product is popular and widely accepted by others can influence attitudes. User-generated content, testimonials, and reviews can serve as social proof, encouraging others to adopt similar attitudes.

Conclusion

Understanding the formation and change of consumer attitudes is essential for effective FMCG marketing. Attitudes, which are shaped by cognitive, affective, and behavioral components, influence consumer perceptions, purchase intentions, and brand loyalty. By employing various strategies such as persuasive communication, credible endorsements, classical conditioning, cognitive dissonance reduction, behavioral influence, and social influence, marketers can effectively change consumer attitudes. These efforts ultimately lead to stronger brand connections, increased customer satisfaction, and sustained market success.

Chapter 6
Personality and Consumer Behavior

Personality significantly influences consumer behavior, shaping preferences, purchasing decisions, and brand loyalty. By understanding the role of personality traits and the concept of brand personality, marketers can develop strategies that resonate with different consumer segments.

The Role of Personality Traits

Personality refers to the unique and consistent patterns of thoughts, feelings, and behaviors that characterize an individual. It influences how people interact with their environment, including their consumption behavior. Key personality theories and traits relevant to consumer behavior include:

1: The Big Five Personality Traits:

Openness to Experience: Individuals high in openness are imaginative, curious, and open to new experiences. They are more likely to try new products and innovative brands. Marketers can target these consumers with novel and unique product offerings.

Conscientiousness: Conscientious individuals are organized, responsible, and goal-oriented. They tend to prefer reliable and high-quality products. Brands that emphasize dependability and effectiveness appeal to this trait.

Extraversion: Extraverts are sociable, energetic, and seek stimulation. They are drawn to products and brands that enhance social experiences and provide excitement. Marketing strategies for this group often involve social events, vibrant advertising, and community engagement.

Agreeableness: Agreeable individuals are cooperative, compassionate, and value harmony. They prefer brands that promote social good and community well-being. Marketers can appeal to this trait by emphasizing ethical practices, sustainability, and community involvement.

Neuroticism: Individuals high in neuroticism are prone to emotional instability and anxiety. They may seek products that offer comfort, security, and stress relief. Brands that position themselves as solutions to these emotional needs can attract neurotic consumers.

2: Other Relevant Personality Traits:

Locus of Control: People with an internal locus of control believe they can influence their outcomes through their actions. They are more likely to engage in informed decision-making and prefer products that align with their sense of control. Conversely, those with an external locus of control feel their outcomes are determined by external factors and may rely more on trusted brands and expert recommendations.

Self-Monitoring: High self-monitors are highly concerned with social appropriateness and adjust their behavior to fit social situations. They are more likely to be influenced by social cues and trends. Low self-monitors are guided by their internal values and preferences, showing greater brand loyalty and consistency in their purchases.

Brand Personality and Consumer Preference

Brand personality refers to the set of human characteristics associated with a brand. It helps consumers relate to brands on a personal level and influences their preferences and loyalty. Key aspects of brand personality and its impact on consumer behavior include:

1: Dimensions of Brand Personality:

Sincerity: Brands characterized by sincerity are perceived as honest, genuine, and trustworthy. Examples include brands that emphasize family values, ethical practices, and transparency. Consumers who value trust and integrity are drawn to sincere brands.

Excitement: Exciting brands are seen as daring, spirited, and imaginative. They appeal to consumers seeking adventure, novelty, and fun. Marketing strategies for exciting brands often involve bold and innovative campaigns, vibrant packaging, and engaging experiences.

Competence: Competent brands are regarded as reliable, intelligent, and successful. They attract consumers who prioritize efficiency, expertise, and quality. Brands that highlight their technical superiority, certifications, and achievements are perceived as competent.

Sophistication: Sophisticated brands are viewed as elegant, prestigious, and classy. They appeal to consumers who aspire to a higher social status and appreciate luxury. Marketing for sophisticated brands often involves premium pricing, exclusive offers, and high-end endorsements.

Ruggedness: Rugged brands are associated with toughness, durability, and outdoorsiness. They attract consumers who value strength and resilience. Marketing strategies for rugged brands emphasize product durability, adventurous lifestyles, and robust design.

2: Building and Communicating Brand Personality:

Consistency in Messaging: Consistent messaging across all marketing channels helps establish a clear and coherent brand personality. This includes the brand's tone of voice, visual identity, and advertising style.

Storytelling: Effective storytelling creates emotional connections with consumers. Brands can share their history, mission, and values through compelling narratives that resonate with their target audience.

Endorsements and Partnerships: Collaborations with celebrities, influencers, and organizations that embody the brand's personality can enhance its credibility and appeal. For example, a fitness brand partnering with a well-known athlete can reinforce its image of competence and ruggedness.

Consumer Engagement: Engaging consumers through social media, events, and interactive campaigns fosters a sense of community and loyalty. Brands that actively listen to and involve their customers in brand-related activities can strengthen their personality and consumer relationships.

3: Impact of Brand Personality on Consumer Preference:

Emotional Connection: Consumers are more likely to prefer and remain loyal to brands with personalities that align with their own self-image and values. Emotional connections foster brand loyalty and advocacy.

Differentiation: A distinctive brand personality helps differentiate a brand from its competitors. In crowded markets, a unique personality can make a brand stand out and attract a specific consumer segment.

Trust and Credibility: Brands with a consistent and authentic personality are perceived as more trustworthy and credible. This trust is crucial for building long-term relationships with consumers.

Purchase Motivation: Brand personality influences purchase motivation by fulfilling consumers' psychological needs. For example, a consumer might choose a sophisticated brand to enhance their self-esteem or an exciting brand to satisfy their need for adventure.

Conclusion

Personality traits significantly influence consumer behavior, shaping preferences, purchasing decisions, and brand loyalty. By understanding the role of personality traits and developing a strong brand personality, FMCG marketers can create strategies that resonate with different consumer segments. A well-defined brand personality fosters emotional connections, differentiation, trust, and purchase motivation, ultimately driving consumer preference and long-term success in the market.

Chapter 7
Lifestyle and Consumer Behavior

Understanding consumer lifestyles is crucial for marketers, particularly in the FMCG sector, where preferences and habits significantly influence purchasing decisions. Lifestyle encompasses a person's activities, interests, opinions, and behaviors, which collectively shape their consumption patterns. This chapter delves into the concept of lifestyle, its impact on consumer behavior, and how lifestyle segmentation can be leveraged in the FMCG industry.

Understanding Consumer Lifestyles

Lifestyle refers to the way individuals live their lives, including their activities, interests, and opinions (AIOs). It reflects their values, attitudes, and social patterns, influencing their consumption behavior and brand preferences.

1: Activities:

Daily Routines: The day-to-day activities, such as work, leisure, exercise, and shopping habits, shape consumer needs and preferences. For example, a busy professional might prefer convenient, ready-to-eat meals.

Hobbies and Interests: Hobbies and interests, such as sports, arts, travel, and technology, can significantly influence purchasing decisions. A fitness enthusiast may prioritize health supplements and athletic wear.

2: Interests:

Social Interests: Social interactions and group affiliations, such as being part of a club, community, or online group, affect consumption patterns. Someone active in environmental groups might prefer eco-friendly products.

Personal Interests: Personal interests, like fashion, gaming, or cooking, can drive specific consumer behaviors and brand loyalties. A fashion-forward individual may frequently buy the latest clothing trends.

3: Opinions:

Self-Perception: How individuals perceive themselves influences their consumption choices. For instance, someone who sees themselves as a trendsetter may seek out unique and innovative products.

Worldview: Opinions on social, political, and environmental issues can shape brand preferences. Consumers who prioritize sustainability might support brands with strong environmental practices.

4: Behavior Patterns:

Spending Habits: Spending habits, such as being frugal or indulgent, directly impact purchase decisions. A budget-conscious consumer might look for discounts and value-for-money products.

Brand Loyalty: Lifestyle influences brand loyalty, with consumers often sticking to brands that align with their lifestyle values and needs.

Lifestyle Segmentation in FMCG

Lifestyle segmentation divides the market into distinct groups based on shared lifestyle characteristics. This approach helps FMCG marketers tailor their products and marketing strategies to meet the specific needs and preferences of different consumer segments.

1: Segmentation Criteria:

Demographics: Age, gender, income, education, and occupation are often combined with lifestyle factors to create more precise segments. For example, young urban professionals might be a distinct segment.

Psychographics: Psychographic segmentation involves understanding consumers' AIOs, personality traits, and values. This deeper insight helps in crafting targeted marketing messages.

Behavioral Patterns: Analyzing purchase behavior, brand loyalty, usage rates, and benefits sought allows for effective segmentation. Frequent buyers of organic products might form a separate segment.

2: Common Lifestyle Segments in FMCG:

Health Conscious Consumers: This segment includes individuals focused on maintaining a healthy lifestyle through diet and exercise. They prefer organic, low-calorie, and nutrient-rich products. Marketing strategies might highlight health benefits, natural ingredients, and endorsements from health experts.

Convenience Seekers: Busy individuals who prioritize convenience in their consumption choices. They look for ready-to-eat meals, quick snacks, and easy-to-use household products. Marketing can emphasize time-saving features and convenience.

Eco-Friendly Consumers: Environmentally conscious consumers prefer products with minimal environmental impact. They seek out sustainable, recyclable, and eco-friendly products. Marketing should focus on the brand's environmental commitment and eco-friendly practices.

Luxury Shoppers: Consumers who indulge in premium and luxury FMCG products. They value exclusivity, quality, and status. Marketing should highlight the premium nature, unique features, and luxury experience of the products.

Tech-Savvy Consumers: Early adopters of technology who seek the latest innovations. They are interested in smart appliances, advanced gadgets, and tech-integrated FMCG products. Marketing can emphasize cutting-edge technology and innovative features.

Family-Oriented Consumers: Families with children who prioritize products that cater to family needs. They look for family-sized packages, safe and child-friendly products. Marketing should focus on safety, family values, and multi-use benefits.

3: Benefits of Lifestyle Segmentation:

Targeted Marketing: By understanding the specific needs and preferences of each segment, marketers can create more targeted and effective marketing campaigns. This leads to better engagement and higher conversion rates.

Product Development: Insights from lifestyle segmentation can guide product development, ensuring that new products align with the lifestyles of target consumers. For example, developing organic baby food for health-conscious, family-oriented consumers.

Enhanced Customer Loyalty: By resonating with consumers on a lifestyle level, brands can build stronger emotional connections and foster customer loyalty. Consumers are more likely to stay loyal to brands that align with their values and lifestyles.

Competitive Advantage: Lifestyle segmentation provides a competitive edge by allowing brands to differentiate themselves in the market. Tailored products and marketing messages help stand out from competitors.

Conclusion

Understanding consumer lifestyles and leveraging lifestyle segmentation are essential for effective FMCG marketing. By analyzing activities, interests, opinions, and behavior patterns, marketers can gain valuable insights into consumer preferences and tailor their strategies accordingly. Lifestyle segmentation allows for more targeted marketing, better product development, enhanced customer loyalty, and a competitive advantage in the market. Ultimately, aligning with consumers' lifestyles leads to stronger brand connections and long-term success in the FMCG industry.

Chapter 8
Consumer Perception of Product Quality

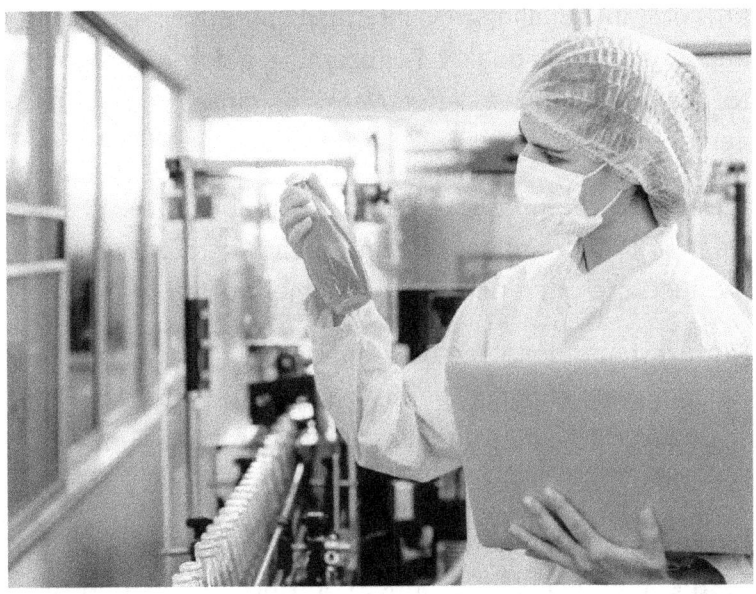

Perception of product quality plays a vital role in shaping consumer behavior, especially in the FMCG sector where competition is fierce and brand loyalty can make a significant difference. Understanding the factors that influence perceived quality and their implications for marketing strategies is crucial for FMCG companies aiming to attract and retain customers.

Factors Influencing Perceived Quality

Perceived quality is the consumer's judgment about a product's overall excellence or superiority. Several factors contribute to how consumers perceive the quality of a product:

1: Intrinsic Attributes:

Performance: The functionality and effectiveness of a product in fulfilling its intended purpose significantly impact perceived quality. For example, a detergent's ability to remove stains effectively enhances its quality perception.

Durability: The product's lifespan and ability to withstand wear and tear influence consumer judgments. Durable products are often perceived as higher quality.

Features: Additional features and benefits beyond the basic function can enhance perceived quality. For instance, a shampoo with added vitamins and minerals may be seen as superior.

Design and Aesthetics: The appearance, design, and aesthetic appeal of a product contribute to its perceived quality. Attractive packaging and product design can elevate consumer perceptions.

2: Extrinsic Attributes:

Brand Name: A well-established and reputable brand name often signals higher quality to consumers. Brands with a strong reputation for quality tend to be trusted more.

Price: Price often serves as a quality indicator, with higher-priced products being perceived as higher quality. However, this perception can vary based on consumer expectations and market positioning.

Packaging: The quality of packaging materials and design can influence perceptions. Premium packaging often suggests a higher quality product inside.

Country of Origin: The origin of a product can affect its perceived quality. Products from certain countries may be associated with higher quality due to their manufacturing standards and reputation.

3: Marketing and Communication:

Advertising and Promotions: Effective advertising that highlights product quality and benefits can shape consumer perceptions. Promotional activities that offer samples or demonstrations can also influence quality perception.

Word of Mouth: Recommendations and reviews from friends, family, and other consumers play a crucial role in shaping perceived quality. Positive word-of-mouth can enhance quality perception.

Public Relations: Media coverage and public relations efforts that emphasize a product's quality attributes can positively impact consumer perceptions.

4: Consumer Expectations and Experiences:

Previous Experience: Personal experiences with a product influence future perceptions of quality. Consistently positive experiences enhance perceived quality, while negative experiences can diminish it.

Expectations: Consumer expectations, formed by past experiences, advertising, and word-of-mouth, affect how they perceive a product's quality. Meeting or exceeding these expectations strengthens quality perception.

Perceived Value: The overall value a consumer perceives in relation to the price paid impacts quality perception. A product that offers good value for money is often seen as higher quality.

Implications for FMCG Marketing

Understanding the factors that influence perceived quality allows FMCG marketers to develop strategies that effectively communicate and enhance the quality perception of their products. Here are some key implications for FMCG marketing:

1: Emphasize Product Features and Benefits:

Highlight Performance and Durability: Marketing messages should emphasize the product's performance and durability. Demonstrations, before-and-after comparisons, and testimonials can effectively showcase these attributes.

Showcase Unique Features: Highlighting unique features and benefits that set the product apart from competitors can enhance perceived quality. This can be done through detailed product descriptions, visual content, and user reviews.

2: Leverage Brand Equity:

Build and Maintain Brand Reputation: Consistently delivering high-quality products and maintaining positive brand equity are essential. Strong brand equity reinforces quality perception and fosters consumer trust.

Brand Extensions: Extending a reputable brand into new product categories can transfer quality perception to new products. However, it's crucial to ensure that the new products meet the brand's established quality standards.

3: Price and Value Communication:

Strategic Pricing: Pricing strategies should reflect the desired quality perception. Premium pricing can signal higher quality, while value pricing can emphasize cost-effectiveness.

Communicate Value Proposition: Clearly communicate the value proposition, highlighting how the product offers superior quality and benefits at a justified price. This can be achieved through advertising, packaging, and point-of-sale materials.

4: Enhance Packaging and Presentation:

Invest in High-Quality Packaging: Premium packaging materials and designs can elevate perceived quality. Packaging should be functional, visually appealing, and reflective of the product's quality attributes.

Eco-Friendly Packaging: For environmentally conscious consumers, eco-friendly packaging can enhance quality perception by aligning with their values.

5: Effective Advertising and Promotions:

Quality-Focused Advertising: Create advertisements that emphasize the product's quality attributes, using credible endorsements, expert opinions, and customer testimonials.

Promotional Activities: Offer samples, demonstrations, and trial offers to allow consumers to experience the product's quality firsthand. This can build confidence and reinforce positive perceptions.

6: Leverage Word of Mouth and Reviews:

Encourage Positive Reviews: Encourage satisfied customers to leave positive reviews and ratings on online platforms. This can be facilitated through follow-up emails, incentives, and easy review submission processes.

Address Negative Feedback: Promptly addressing negative feedback and resolving customer issues can mitigate negative perceptions and demonstrate a commitment to quality.

7: Public Relations and Media Coverage:

Quality Stories: Use public relations to share stories about the product's quality, including its manufacturing process, quality control measures, and any awards or certifications received.

Media Endorsements: Gaining endorsements from credible media sources can enhance perceived quality. Press releases, media events, and influencer partnerships can help achieve this.

Conclusion

Perceived product quality is a critical determinant of consumer behavior in the FMCG sector. By understanding the intrinsic and extrinsic factors that influence quality perception, marketers can develop effective strategies to enhance and communicate their product's quality attributes. Emphasizing product features, leveraging brand equity, strategic pricing, investing in packaging, effective advertising, leveraging word of mouth, and utilizing public relations are all essential components of a comprehensive approach to managing and enhancing perceived quality. These efforts ultimately lead to stronger brand loyalty, increased consumer trust, and long-term success in the competitive FMCG market.

Chapter 9
Brand Loyalty and Brand Equity

Brand loyalty and brand equity are fundamental concepts in marketing, particularly in the FMCG sector where consumer retention and strong brand presence are critical for long-term success. This chapter explores the strategies for building brand loyalty and the methods for measuring brand equity in the FMCG industry.

Building Brand Loyalty in FMCG

Brand loyalty refers to consumers' consistent preference for one brand over others, leading to repeated purchases and a lower likelihood of switching to competitors. Building brand loyalty involves creating a positive and memorable consumer experience that fosters trust and emotional connections.

1: Quality Consistency:

Delivering Consistent Quality: Consistently providing high-quality products is essential for building trust and loyalty. Consumers need to feel confident that they will receive the same level of quality with each purchase.

Quality Control Measures: Implementing strict quality control measures ensures that the products meet or exceed consumer expectations every time.

2: Customer Engagement and Communication:

Personalized Communication: Personalized marketing messages and offers tailored to individual consumer preferences can enhance the connection between the brand and the consumer.

Feedback Mechanisms: Providing channels for consumer feedback and actively responding to it demonstrates that the brand values its customers' opinions and is committed to improvement.

3: Loyalty Programs and Incentives:

Rewards Programs: Implementing loyalty programs that offer rewards, discounts, or exclusive offers for repeat purchases can incentivize continued patronage.

Referral Programs: Encouraging existing customers to refer new ones through referral programs can expand the customer base while rewarding loyal consumers.

4: Emotional Branding:

Building Emotional Connections: Creating an emotional connection with consumers through storytelling, brand values, and community engagement fosters loyalty. Brands that resonate with consumers' personal values and emotions are more likely to be chosen repeatedly.

Brand Personality: Developing a distinct brand personality that consumers can relate to and identify with helps in forming a strong emotional bond.

5: Convenience and Accessibility:

Ease of Purchase: Ensuring that the product is easily accessible through multiple channels, including online and offline retail, enhances convenience and encourages repeat purchases.

Customer Service: Providing excellent customer service at all touchpoints, from purchase to post-purchase support, reinforces positive experiences and loyalty.

6: Innovation and Adaptation:

Continuous Innovation: Regularly introducing new products, flavors, or variations keeps the brand relevant and exciting for consumers.

Adaptation to Trends: Staying attuned to market trends and consumer preferences allows the brand to adapt and meet changing demands effectively.

Measuring Brand Equity

Brand equity refers to the value a brand adds to a product, encompassing consumer perceptions, attitudes, and loyalty. Measuring brand equity is crucial for understanding the brand's strength and guiding strategic decisions.

1: Brand Awareness:

Top-of-Mind Awareness (TOMA): Measuring the extent to which a brand is the first that comes to consumers' minds when thinking of a product category.

Brand Recall and Recognition: Assessing how easily consumers can recall or recognize the brand in various contexts, including in advertising and on store shelves.

2: Brand Associations:

Brand Image: Evaluating the associations and attributes consumers link with the brand, such as quality, reliability, and innovation.

Emotional Associations: Understanding the emotional connections and feelings consumers have toward the brand, such as trust, excitement, or nostalgia.

3: Perceived Quality:

Consumer Perceptions: Measuring consumers' perceptions of the brand's quality compared to competitors.

Product Performance: Assessing the perceived performance and reliability of the brand's products.

4: Brand Loyalty:

Repeat Purchase Rate: Tracking the percentage of consumers who repeatedly purchase the brand's products.

Customer Retention Rate: Measuring the rate at which customers remain loyal to the brand over time.

5: Brand Valuation:

Financial Performance: Analyzing financial metrics such as market share, revenue growth, and profitability attributable to the brand.

Market Position: Evaluating the brand's position in the market relative to competitors, including its competitive advantages and strengths.

6: Brand Advocacy:

Net Promoter Score (NPS): Measuring the likelihood that consumers would recommend the brand to others, indicating overall satisfaction and loyalty.

Social Media Sentiment: Analyzing consumer sentiment and engagement on social media platforms to gauge brand advocacy and public perception.

7: Customer-Based Brand Equity (CBBE):

Keller's Brand Equity Model: Utilizing the CBBE model, which focuses on building a strong brand by ensuring brand salience, performance, imagery, judgments, feelings, and resonance.

Brand Resonance: Measuring the depth of consumer relationships with the brand, including loyalty, attachment, community, and engagement.

Implications for FMCG Marketing

1: Strategic Brand Positioning:

Differentiation: Positioning the brand uniquely in the market to stand out from competitors and resonate with target consumers.

Value Proposition: Clearly communicating the unique value proposition that the brand offers to consumers, emphasizing benefits and strengths.

2: Marketing Mix Optimization:

Product: Ensuring the product meets consumer needs and expectations in terms of quality, features, and design.

Price: Setting prices that reflect the perceived value and quality of the brand while remaining competitive.

Place: Distributing products through convenient and accessible channels to maximize reach and availability.

Promotion: Utilizing integrated marketing communications to consistently convey the brand message across all touchpoints.

3: Brand Equity Management:

Monitoring and Measurement: Regularly measuring brand equity to track progress, identify areas for improvement, and guide strategic decisions.

Brand Reinforcement: Continuously reinforcing the brand's strengths and maintaining consistency in brand messaging and experience.

4: Consumer-Centric Approach:

Understanding Consumer Needs: Conducting market research to understand consumer preferences, behaviors, and needs.

Engaging Consumers: Actively engaging with consumers through various channels, including social media, events, and direct interactions, to build and maintain strong relationships.

Conclusion

Building brand loyalty and measuring brand equity are essential for sustaining success in the competitive FMCG market. By delivering consistent quality, engaging customers, offering loyalty programs, building emotional connections, and ensuring convenience, FMCG brands can foster strong loyalty among consumers. Measuring brand equity through awareness, associations, perceived quality, loyalty, valuation, advocacy, and the CBBE model provides valuable insights for strategic decision-making. These efforts ultimately enhance the brand's market position, drive consumer preference, and ensure long-term profitability and growth.

Chapter 10
Pricing and Consumer Behavior

Pricing plays a crucial role in consumer behavior, especially in the FMCG sector where price sensitivity can significantly influence purchasing decisions. Understanding how consumers perceive prices and applying psychological pricing strategies can help FMCG companies optimize their pricing models to attract and retain customers.

Price Perception and Sensitivity

Price perception refers to how consumers view and interpret the price of a product, which can be influenced by various factors. Price sensitivity, on the other hand, measures how changes in price affect consumer demand for a product.

1: Factors Influencing Price Perception:

Reference Prices: Consumers often have a reference price in mind, which is based on their previous experiences, knowledge, and expectations. If the actual price is lower than the reference price, consumers perceive the product as a good deal.

Price-Quality Relationship: Many consumers associate higher prices with higher quality. This perception can lead them to prefer higher-priced products, assuming they are of better quality.

Price Transparency: Clear and transparent pricing helps consumers make informed decisions and trust the brand. Hidden fees or unclear pricing can negatively affect price perception.

Promotional Context: Discounts, sales, and promotions can influence how consumers perceive the regular price of a product. A product on sale may be seen as a better value.

Brand Image: The overall image and reputation of a brand can impact how its prices are perceived. Premium brands can often charge higher prices without negatively affecting consumer perception.

2: Price Sensitivity:

Elasticity of Demand: Price sensitivity is measured through price elasticity of demand, which shows how demand changes with price variations. Products with high price elasticity see significant demand changes with price fluctuations, while inelastic products have stable demand despite price changes.

Income Levels: Consumers with higher disposable incomes are generally less price-sensitive, while those with lower incomes are more sensitive to price changes.

Substitutes Availability: The presence of substitute products increases price sensitivity as consumers can easily switch to alternatives if the price rises.

Product Necessity: Essential goods, such as basic food items, tend to have lower price sensitivity compared to non-essential or luxury goods.

Purchase Frequency: Frequently purchased items often face higher price sensitivity since consumers are more aware of price changes and their cumulative cost impact.

Psychological Pricing Strategies

Psychological pricing strategies leverage consumers' behavioral tendencies and perceptions to influence their purchasing decisions. These strategies can make prices more appealing and encourage sales.

1: Charm Pricing (Odd-Even Pricing):

Odd Pricing: Setting prices slightly below a round number, such as $9.99 instead of $10, creates a perception of getting a deal. Consumers tend to focus on the first digit and perceive the price as lower.

Even Pricing: For high-end products, even pricing (e.g., $100) can convey quality and exclusivity, appealing to consumers seeking premium products.

2: Prestige Pricing:

Premium Pricing: Setting higher prices to create an image of quality and exclusivity. This strategy works well for luxury and premium products where consumers equate high price with high quality.

Psychological Impact: High prices can attract status-conscious consumers who associate the product with prestige and superior quality.

2: Bundling and Unbundling:

Product Bundling: Selling multiple products together at a lower price than if purchased separately can increase perceived value and encourage consumers to buy more. For example, a shampoo and conditioner bundle.

Unbundling: Offering products separately can cater to consumers who prefer to buy only what they need, potentially allowing for higher overall pricing flexibility.

3: Price Anchoring:

Reference Points: Presenting a high initial price (anchor) and then offering a discount or a lower-priced alternative makes the latter appear more attractive. For instance, showing a $100 item discounted to $70 makes the $70 price seem like a better deal.

Comparison Sets: Displaying multiple products with varying prices side by side can guide consumers towards a middle option, which appears more reasonable compared to the extremes.

4: Decoy Pricing:

Creating a Decoy: Introducing a higher-priced, less attractive option (decoy) to make other options appear more reasonable or attractive. For example, a small popcorn for $3, a medium for $6.50, and a large for $7. The medium size may be seen as poor value compared to the large, encouraging consumers to choose the large.

5: Loss Leader Pricing:

Attracting Customers: Selling certain products at a loss to attract customers into the store, hoping they will purchase additional items at regular prices. This strategy is common in supermarkets and retail stores.

Cross-Selling Opportunities: Once in the store, customers are likely to purchase other items, compensating for the loss on the leader item.

6: Psychological Discounting:

Perceived Savings: Offering discounts with a percentage off (e.g., 20% off) can be more appealing than a dollar amount off, even if the actual savings are the same.

Limited-Time Offers: Creating a sense of urgency with time-limited discounts encourages immediate purchases, leveraging consumers' fear of missing out (FOMO).

7: Tiered Pricing:

Multiple Price Points: Offering products at different price points to cater to various segments of consumers. This can include basic, standard, and premium versions of a product.

Consumer Choice: Providing multiple options allows consumers to choose based on their budget and perceived value, often leading them to select the middle option.

Implications for FMCG Marketing

1: Targeted Pricing Strategies:

Segment-Specific Pricing: Tailoring pricing strategies to different consumer segments based on their price sensitivity, purchasing behavior, and preferences.

Geographic Pricing: Adjusting prices based on geographic locations, considering local economic conditions, competition, and consumer purchasing power.

2: Promotional Tactics:

Seasonal Discounts: Offering discounts during specific seasons or holidays can boost sales and attract price-sensitive consumers.

Loyalty Rewards: Implementing loyalty programs that offer special discounts or rewards for repeat purchases helps retain customers and build brand loyalty.

3: Dynamic Pricing:

Real-Time Adjustments: Using technology to adjust prices in real-time based on demand, competition, and inventory levels. This approach is common in e-commerce and can maximize revenue.

Personalized Pricing: Leveraging data analytics to offer personalized pricing and discounts based on individual consumer behavior and preferences.

4: Price Communication:

Transparent Pricing: Clearly communicating prices and any additional costs to build trust and avoid negative perceptions.

Value Messaging: Emphasizing the value and benefits of the product rather than just the price, helping consumers see the overall worth of their purchase.

Conclusion

Understanding price perception and sensitivity is crucial for developing effective pricing strategies in the FMCG sector. By leveraging psychological pricing techniques, FMCG companies can influence consumer behavior, attract price-sensitive consumers, and enhance perceived value. Implementing targeted pricing strategies, dynamic pricing models, and transparent communication helps build consumer trust and loyalty, ultimately driving sales and long-term success.

Chapter 11
Promotions and Consumer Behavior

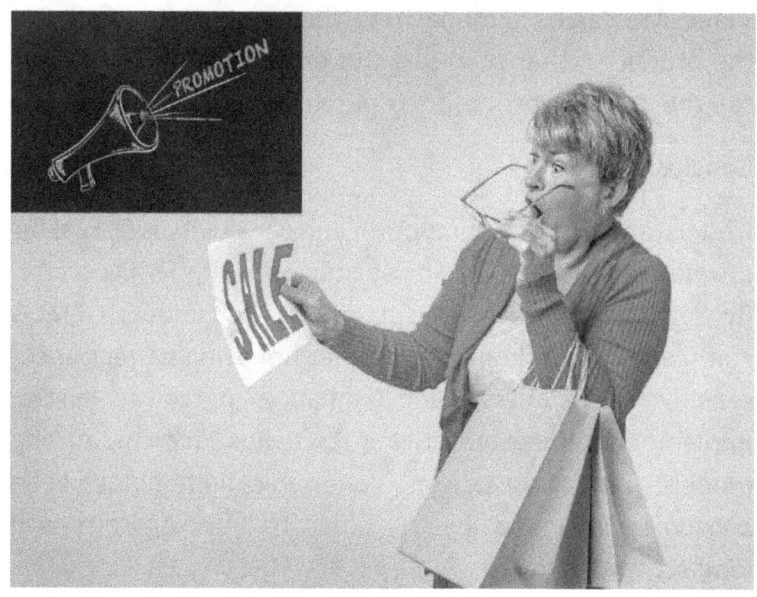

Promotions are a critical aspect of marketing in the FMCG sector. They significantly influence consumer behavior by driving awareness, encouraging trial, and ultimately fostering brand loyalty. This chapter explores the impact of promotions on consumer decisions and examines various promotional strategies that FMCG companies can employ to achieve their marketing objectives.

Impact of Promotions on Consumer Decisions

Promotions can have a profound effect on consumer behavior and decision-making processes. They serve multiple purposes, from attracting new customers to rewarding loyal ones. Here are some key impacts:

1: Increased Brand Awareness:

Attention-Grabbing: Promotions, especially those that are well-publicized, grab consumers' attention and increase brand visibility.

Trial Encouragement: Offering promotions such as discounts or samples can encourage consumers to try a new product they might not have considered otherwise.

2: Perceived Value Enhancement:

Discounts and Deals: Promotions that offer discounts or additional value for the same price (e.g., buy one get one free) can enhance the perceived value of a product.

Bundling: Bundling products together at a discounted rate can make the overall purchase seem like a better deal, enhancing the perceived value.

3: Purchase Acceleration:

Limited-Time Offers: Time-sensitive promotions create a sense of urgency, prompting consumers to make quicker purchasing decisions to avoid missing out.

Stockpiling: Promotions on frequently used items can encourage consumers to buy in bulk, increasing short-term sales.

4: Brand Switching:

Competitive Promotions: Promotions can entice consumers to switch from their regular brand to try a competitor's product, especially if the offer is compelling.

Sampling and Trials: Free samples or trial offers lower the risk for consumers in trying a new brand, facilitating brand switching.

5: Increased Consumption:

Larger Quantities: Promotions that encourage bulk purchases can lead to increased consumption as consumers have more of the product on hand.

Usage Expansion: Promotional campaigns that educate consumers about new uses for a product can increase consumption by expanding its applications.

6: Customer Loyalty and Retention:

Reward Programs: Promotions targeting existing customers, such as loyalty programs, can enhance customer retention and build long-term loyalty.

Personalized Offers: Tailored promotions that cater to individual preferences can strengthen the relationship between the brand and its consumers.

Promotional Strategies in FMCG

Effective promotional strategies are essential for FMCG companies to capture and maintain consumer interest. Here are several promotional strategies commonly used in the FMCG sector:

1: Price Promotions:

Discounts and Coupons: Offering price reductions or coupons is one of the most straightforward and effective ways to attract consumers and boost sales.

Rebates: Providing a rebate on a product can entice consumers to purchase while giving them the perception of getting a better deal.

2: Product Promotions:

Buy One Get One Free (BOGOF): This strategy encourages consumers to buy more by offering a free product with the purchase of another.

Sampling: Distributing free samples allows consumers to try the product without financial risk, increasing the likelihood of future purchases.

3: Value-Added Promotions:

Bundling: Combining products into a package deal at a reduced price can enhance the perceived value and encourage consumers to purchase multiple items.

Gifts with Purchase: Offering a free gift with the purchase of a product can enhance the attractiveness of the deal and incentivize purchases.

4: Loyalty Programs:

Points Systems: Rewarding consumers with points for every purchase that can be redeemed for discounts or free products encourages repeat purchases.

Exclusive Offers: Providing special deals or early access to new products for loyalty program members strengthens customer loyalty.

5: Contests and Sweepstakes:

Engagement Campaigns: Running contests or sweepstakes can generate excitement and engagement, encouraging consumers to participate and share their experiences.

Prize Incentives: Offering attractive prizes for contest winners can drive participation and increase brand visibility.

6: Seasonal and Event-Based Promotions:

Holiday Promotions: Leveraging holidays and special occasions with themed promotions can drive sales and create a festive shopping atmosphere.

Event Sponsorships: Sponsoring events or creating promotions around major events (e.g., sports, concerts) can enhance brand exposure and connect with consumers on an emotional level.

7: Digital Promotions:

Social Media Campaigns: Utilizing social media platforms to run promotional campaigns can reach a broad audience and foster interaction with the brand.

Email Marketing: Sending targeted promotional emails to consumers based on their preferences and purchase history can drive engagement and sales.

8: In-Store Promotions:

Point-of-Sale Displays: Attractive in-store displays and promotions can capture consumer attention and drive impulse purchases.

Demos and Tastings: Offering live demonstrations or tastings in-store can provide a hands-on experience, encouraging consumers to try and buy the product.

Implications for FMCG Marketing

1: Strategic Planning:

Consumer Insights: Understanding consumer behavior, preferences, and trends is crucial for designing effective promotional strategies. Market research and data analytics can provide valuable insights.

Goal Setting: Clearly defining the objectives of promotional campaigns, such as increasing brand awareness, driving sales, or enhancing loyalty, helps in planning and execution.

2: Integration with Marketing Mix:

Coordinated Efforts: Promotions should be integrated with other elements of the marketing mix, including product, price, place, and advertising, to ensure consistency and maximize impact.

Cross-Promotions: Collaborating with complementary brands for cross-promotions can expand reach and attract new customers.

3: Monitoring and Evaluation:

Performance Metrics: Tracking key performance indicators (KPIs) such as sales lift, redemption rates, and return on investment (ROI) helps in evaluating the effectiveness of promotions.

Feedback and Adaptation: Collecting consumer feedback and analyzing promotion outcomes allows for continuous improvement and adaptation of strategies.

4: Consumer-Centric Approach:

Personalization: Personalizing promotions based on consumer behavior and preferences can enhance relevance and effectiveness.

Value Proposition: Ensuring that promotions align with the brand's value proposition and enhance the overall consumer experience is crucial for long-term success.

Conclusion

Promotions are a powerful tool in the FMCG marketer's arsenal, capable of significantly influencing consumer behavior and driving business success. By understanding the impact of promotions on consumer decisions and employing a variety of promotional strategies, FMCG companies can attract new customers, retain existing ones, and boost sales. Strategic planning, integration with the marketing mix, monitoring and evaluation, and a consumer-centric approach are essential for creating effective and impactful promotional campaigns.

Through well-designed promotions, FMCG brands can enhance their market presence, foster brand loyalty, and achieve sustainable growth.

Chapter 12
Packaging and Visual Appeal

Packaging is a critical element in the marketing and presentation of FMCG products. It serves not only as a protective container but also as a vital communication tool that can influence consumer perceptions and purchasing decisions. This chapter explores the importance of packaging in the FMCG sector and delves into the psychological aspects of packaging design.

Importance of Packaging in FMCG

1: Protection and Preservation:

Product Safety: Packaging ensures that the product reaches the consumer in optimal condition by protecting it from physical damage, contamination, and spoilage.

Shelf Life Extension: Proper packaging can extend the shelf life of perishable goods by protecting them from environmental factors such as light, moisture, and air.

2: Convenience and Functionality:

Ease of Use: Packaging designed for convenience, such as resealable bags, easy-open lids, and portion-sized packs, enhances the user experience.

Portability: For on-the-go consumers, portable and easy-to-carry packaging is crucial. This is especially important in categories like snacks and beverages.

3: Brand Identity and Recognition:

Visual Branding: Packaging is often the first point of contact between the consumer and the brand. Consistent use of brand colors, logos, and imagery helps in building brand identity and recognition.

Differentiation: In a crowded market, unique packaging design helps products stand out on the shelves and attracts consumer attention.

4: Communication and Information:

Product Information: Packaging communicates essential information such as ingredients, usage instructions, nutritional facts, and expiration dates.

Brand Messaging: Packaging serves as a medium for conveying the brand's story, values, and promises, helping to build an emotional connection with consumers.

5: Sustainability and Environmental Impact:

Eco-Friendly Packaging: As consumers become more environmentally conscious, sustainable packaging options can influence purchasing decisions. Brands that use recyclable, biodegradable, or reusable packaging can attract eco-conscious consumers.

Corporate Responsibility: Sustainable packaging demonstrates a brand's commitment to environmental responsibility, enhancing its reputation and appeal.

Psychological Aspects of Packaging Design

Packaging design can significantly influence consumer behavior by appealing to their emotions, perceptions, and cognitive biases. Here are some psychological aspects of packaging design:

1: Color Psychology:

Emotional Impact: Colors evoke specific emotions and associations. For example, red can create a sense of urgency and excitement, blue can convey trust and calmness, and green is often associated with health and sustainability.

Brand Association: Consistent use of brand colors helps reinforce brand identity and makes products easily recognizable on the shelves.

2: Shape and Form:

Attention-Grabbing Shapes: Unique and unconventional shapes can attract consumer attention and differentiate the product from competitors.

Ergonomics: Shapes that are easy to hold and use enhance consumer satisfaction and can influence purchasing decisions.

3: Typography and Imagery:

Readability: Clear and readable typography is crucial for conveying product information effectively. Fonts that are easy to read at a glance are preferred for FMCG products.

Visual Appeal: High-quality images and graphics can make the product more appealing and help convey its benefits. For example, images of fresh fruits on a juice carton can suggest freshness and quality.

4: Material and Texture:

Tactile Experience: The material and texture of packaging can influence consumer perceptions. Matte finishes may convey sophistication, while glossy finishes can suggest luxury.

Eco-Friendliness: The choice of materials, such as biodegradable or recycled content, can appeal to environmentally conscious consumers.

5: Transparency and Visibility:

Product Visibility: Transparent packaging allows consumers to see the product inside, which can increase trust and reduce uncertainty.

Window Designs: Strategically placed windows on packaging can highlight the quality and appeal of the product.

6: Imagery and Iconography:

Product Representation: Visuals on the packaging should accurately represent the product to set correct expectations and avoid disappointment.

Icons and Symbols: Easily recognizable icons and symbols can communicate product benefits quickly, such as "gluten-free," "organic," or "low-calorie."

7: Messaging and Claims:

Clear Messaging: Simple and clear messaging helps consumers quickly understand the product's benefits and features.

Credibility: Authentic claims and endorsements, such as certifications and awards, can build trust and credibility.

Implications for FMCG Marketing

1: Holistic Design Approach:

Integrated Branding: Ensure that packaging design aligns with the overall brand strategy and marketing messages to create a cohesive brand experience.

Consumer Insights: Conduct research to understand consumer preferences and behaviors, using these insights to inform packaging design.

2: Innovative Packaging Solutions:

Design Innovation: Stay ahead of trends and innovate in packaging design to capture consumer interest and differentiate from competitors.

Functionality and Aesthetics: Balance functionality with visual appeal to create packaging that is both practical and attractive.

3: Sustainability Initiatives:

Eco-Friendly Practices: Invest in sustainable packaging solutions to meet the growing demand for environmentally responsible products.

Consumer Education: Educate consumers about the sustainability efforts and benefits of the packaging to enhance brand perception.

4: Testing and Feedback:

Prototype Testing: Test packaging prototypes with target consumers to gather feedback and make necessary adjustments before full-scale production.

Continuous Improvement: Regularly review and update packaging designs based on consumer feedback, market trends, and technological advancements.

Conclusion

Packaging in the FMCG sector is a multifaceted tool that extends beyond mere product protection. It plays a vital role in shaping consumer perceptions, influencing purchasing decisions, and reinforcing brand identity. By understanding the importance of packaging and leveraging the psychological aspects of design, FMCG companies can create packaging that not only attracts consumers but also builds loyalty and drives sales.

Sustainable and innovative packaging solutions further enhance brand appeal and meet the evolving demands of environmentally conscious consumers. Through strategic packaging design, FMCG brands can achieve a competitive edge and ensure long-term success in the market.

Chapter 13
Consumer Decision Heuristics

Consumers often use mental shortcuts, known as heuristics, to simplify decision-making processes, especially when faced with numerous choices in the FMCG sector. These heuristics help consumers make quick and efficient decisions but can also lead to biases and suboptimal choices. This chapter explores the types of decision-making shortcuts and delves into the phenomenon of impulse buying behavior.

Types of Decision-Making Shortcuts

1: Price-Quality Heuristic:

Perception of Value: Consumers often equate higher prices with better quality. This heuristic simplifies the evaluation process by assuming that more expensive products are superior.

Brand Premium: Premium brands leverage this heuristic to justify higher prices, positioning themselves as high-quality options in the market.

2: Brand Loyalty Heuristic:

Trust and Familiarity: Consumers tend to stick with brands they know and trust. This loyalty reduces the cognitive effort required to evaluate new options.

Habitual Purchasing: Repeated positive experiences with a brand reinforce loyalty, making consumers less likely to switch even when alternatives are available.

3: Country-of-Origin Heuristic:

National Stereotypes: Consumers often associate certain qualities with products from specific countries. For instance, German engineering is perceived as reliable, and Swiss watches as high-quality.

Patriotism and Ethnocentrism: Some consumers prefer products from their own country, driven by national pride or the belief that domestic products are superior.

4: Scarcity Heuristic:

Limited Availability: Products perceived as scarce or limited edition are often seen as more valuable, prompting quicker purchase decisions.

Fear of Missing Out (FOMO): Scarcity creates urgency, leveraging consumers' fear of missing out on exclusive products or deals.

5: Social Proof Heuristic:

Popularity and Reviews: Consumers often look to others for cues on what to buy. High ratings, positive reviews, and popular products are more likely to be chosen.

Influencer Endorsements: Recommendations from trusted figures or influencers can significantly sway purchasing decisions.

6: Authority Heuristic:

Expert Opinions: Endorsements from experts or authoritative figures can influence consumer choices, as these opinions are perceived as credible and knowledgeable.

Certifications and Awards: Products with certifications or awards are often chosen over uncertified options, assuming higher quality or safety standards.

7: Anchoring Heuristic:

Initial Price Anchors: Consumers rely heavily on the first piece of information (anchor) they receive. An initial high price can make subsequent discounts appear more attractive.

Comparison Shopping: Price comparisons with similar products anchor consumers' perceptions of value and affordability.

8: Simplicity Heuristic:

Ease of Use: Products that are simple to understand and use are preferred, reducing the cognitive load on consumers.

Minimalist Packaging: Clear and straightforward packaging designs are often perceived as more trustworthy and user-friendly.

Impulse Buying Behavior

Impulse buying is a spontaneous and unplanned purchase triggered by external stimuli. This behavior is prevalent in the FMCG sector due to the nature of the products and the shopping environment. Here are key factors and psychological mechanisms behind impulse buying:

1: Environmental Cues:

Store Layout and Display: Strategic product placement, such as items near checkout counters or at eye level, can trigger impulse buys.

Atmospherics: Elements like lighting, music, and scents can create a shopping environment conducive to impulse purchases.

2: Emotional Triggers:

Mood Enhancement: Consumers often indulge in impulse buying to elevate their mood or as a form of self-reward.

Stress Relief: Shopping can serve as a coping mechanism for stress, leading to impulsive purchases.

3: Marketing and Promotions:

Limited-Time Offers: Flash sales, discounts, and limited-time offers create urgency and encourage immediate purchases.

In-Store Promotions: Samples, demonstrations, and promotional displays can spur impulse buying by highlighting new or attractive products.

4: Product Characteristics:

Appealing Packaging: Visually attractive and eye-catching packaging can draw attention and prompt impulsive decisions.

Novelty and Innovation: New and innovative products often entice consumers to buy on impulse, driven by curiosity or the desire to try something different.

5: Personal Factors:

Impulsivity Trait: Some individuals are naturally more impulsive and prone to making spontaneous purchases.

Financial Flexibility: Consumers with disposable income or low financial constraints are more likely to indulge in impulse buying.

Implications for FMCG Marketing

1: Leveraging Heuristics:

Highlighting Quality: Emphasize product quality through pricing, packaging, and brand messaging to leverage the price-quality heuristic.

Building Brand Loyalty: Foster trust and loyalty through consistent quality, customer engagement, and loyalty programs.

2: Creating Urgency and Scarcity:

Limited Editions: Introduce limited-edition products to create a sense of scarcity and exclusivity.

Time-Sensitive Promotions: Use flash sales and time-limited discounts to encourage immediate purchases.

3: Enhancing Store Environment:

Strategic Placement: Position impulse-buy items near checkout counters and high-traffic areas.

Sensory Appeal: Use lighting, music, and scents to create an inviting shopping atmosphere that encourages impulse buying.

4: Utilizing Social Proof and Authority:

Customer Reviews: Highlight positive reviews and ratings on packaging and in-store displays.

Expert Endorsements: Secure endorsements from trusted experts or influencers to build credibility.

5: Simplifying Decision-Making:

Clear Messaging: Use simple and clear packaging designs that make it easy for consumers to understand the product.

Comparison Charts: Provide comparison charts or key benefit highlights to aid in quick decision-making.

6: Emotional Marketing:

Storytelling: Use emotional storytelling in marketing campaigns to create a connection with consumers and encourage impulse purchases.

Mood-Enhancing Products: Promote products that are associated with mood enhancement or stress relief.

Conclusion

Understanding consumer decision heuristics and impulse buying behavior is crucial for FMCG marketers. By leveraging these psychological insights, companies can design more effective marketing strategies, optimize product placement, and create compelling promotional campaigns. Recognizing the various heuristics consumers use to simplify their decision-making processes and the triggers that lead to impulse buying can help FMCG brands capture consumer interest, drive sales, and build long-term loyalty. Through strategic application of these insights, FMCG marketers can create a more engaging and persuasive shopping experience that resonates with consumers' cognitive and emotional needs.

Chapter 14
Cross-Cultural Consumer Behavior

Understanding cross-cultural consumer behavior is essential for FMCG companies operating in a global market. Cultural differences significantly impact consumer preferences, purchasing behaviors, and brand perceptions. This chapter explores cultural variations in FMCG consumption and offers strategies for adapting marketing approaches to succeed in diverse international markets.

Cultural Differences in FMCG Consumption

1: Consumption Patterns:

Food Preferences: Dietary habits vary widely across cultures. For instance, rice is a staple in many Asian countries, while bread is more common in Western diets.

Local food preferences must be considered when marketing FMCG products.

Health and Wellness: Attitudes towards health and wellness can influence product choices. Some cultures prioritize organic and natural products, while others may focus more on convenience and price.

Product Usage: Cultural norms dictate how products are used. For example, in some countries, people prefer powdered detergent over liquid detergent due to water quality or washing habits.

2: Brand Perception and Loyalty:

Local vs. Global Brands: In some cultures, local brands are preferred for their perceived authenticity and cultural relevance. In others, global brands are seen as superior due to their international reputation.

Trust and Reliability: Trust in brands varies; some cultures place high importance on brand reputation and longevity, while others may be more open to trying new brands.

3: Shopping Behavior:

Purchase Channels: The prevalence of online versus offline shopping can differ. For example, e-commerce is highly developed in China, while traditional retail is still dominant in many parts of Africa.

Frequency and Volume: Shopping frequency and the volume of purchases can vary. In some cultures, bulk buying is common, while in others, consumers shop more frequently for smaller quantities.

4: Price Sensitivity and Value Perception:

Economic Factors: Price sensitivity can be influenced by economic conditions. In developing countries, consumers may prioritize affordability, while in wealthier nations, consumers might be willing to pay a premium for quality.

Value Perception: The concept of value can differ. For instance, in some cultures, value is equated with product quantity, while in others, it's associated with premium quality or brand prestige.

5: Advertising and Communication:

Language and Messaging: Effective communication requires understanding language nuances and cultural connotations. What works in one culture may not resonate in another.

Advertising Channels: Preferred advertising channels can vary. In some regions, television remains a dominant medium, while in others, digital and social media have a greater impact.

Adapting Marketing Strategies Globally

1: Market Research and Cultural Insights:

Local Understanding: Conduct thorough market research to gain deep insights into local consumer behavior, preferences, and cultural norms.

Cultural Sensitivity: Develop cultural sensitivity by engaging with local experts and stakeholders who understand the nuances of the market.

2: Product Adaptation:

Customization: Adapt products to meet local tastes and preferences. This can include modifying flavors, ingredients, packaging sizes, and usage instructions.

Innovation: Introduce new products that cater specifically to the needs and preferences of local markets.

3: Brand Positioning:

Local Branding: Consider using local branding strategies to build trust and relevance. This can involve collaborating with local influencers or celebrities.

Global Consistency: Maintain a balance between local adaptation and global brand consistency to ensure the brand's core identity remains intact.

4: Pricing Strategies:

Localized Pricing: Adjust pricing strategies based on local economic conditions and consumer price sensitivity. This may involve offering a range of product tiers to cater to different income levels.

Promotions and Discounts: Tailor promotions and discount strategies to align with local shopping habits and festive seasons.

5: Distribution Channels:

Retail Partnerships: Form partnerships with local retailers and distributors who understand the market and have established networks.

E-commerce Integration: Leverage the growing trend of online shopping by establishing a strong e-commerce presence, especially in markets where digital adoption is high.

6: Advertising and Communication:

Localized Campaigns: Develop advertising campaigns that resonate with local cultural values, traditions, and humor.

Multilingual Content: Ensure marketing content is available in local languages and dialects to improve accessibility and relatability.

7: Cultural Sensitivity in Marketing:

Avoiding Stereotypes: Be mindful of cultural stereotypes and avoid reinforcing them in marketing campaigns. Strive for authenticity and respect.

Inclusive Representation: Represent diverse cultural groups in marketing materials to foster inclusivity and relatability.

8: Building Trust and Relationships:

Community Engagement: Engage with local communities through corporate social responsibility (CSR) initiatives and local events to build goodwill and brand loyalty.

Customer Feedback: Actively seek and incorporate customer feedback to continuously improve products and marketing strategies based on local preferences.

Case Studies: Successful Cross-Cultural Marketing

1: McDonald's:

Local Menus: McDonald's adapts its menu to suit local tastes. In India, it offers vegetarian options like the McAloo Tikki, while in Japan, it has the Teriyaki Burger.

Cultural Celebrations: The brand often aligns its promotions with local festivals and holidays, such as the Lunar New Year in China.

2: Coca-Cola:

Personalized Campaigns: Coca-Cola's "Share a Coke" campaign personalized bottles with popular names in different countries, resonating with local consumers.

Local Collaborations: The brand collaborates with local artists and influencers to create culturally relevant marketing content.

3: Unilever:

Dove Campaigns: Dove's "Real Beauty" campaign was tailored to celebrate diverse beauty standards in different regions, emphasizing inclusivity and cultural sensitivity.

Lifebuoy Initiatives: Lifebuoy soap runs hygiene education programs in developing countries, addressing local health issues and building brand trust.

Conclusion

Cross-cultural consumer behavior is complex and multifaceted, requiring FMCG companies to adopt a nuanced and flexible approach to marketing.

By understanding cultural differences in FMCG consumption and adapting marketing strategies accordingly, brands can effectively engage with diverse consumer bases and achieve global success. The key lies in balancing local adaptation with global brand consistency, leveraging cultural insights, and fostering strong relationships with local communities. Through thoughtful and culturally sensitive marketing strategies, FMCG companies can build lasting connections with consumers worldwide, driving brand loyalty and growth.

Chapter 15
Consumer Emotions and Purchasing Decisions

Emotions play a pivotal role in shaping consumer behavior and purchasing decisions, particularly in the FMCG sector where choices are frequent and varied. This chapter delves into the emotional triggers that influence FMCG marketing and explores effective emotional branding strategies that can resonate with consumers on a deeper level.

Emotional Triggers in FMCG Marketing

1: Happiness and Joy:

Positive Associations: FMCG brands often aim to create associations with happiness and joy. This can be achieved through cheerful advertising, uplifting messages, and the promotion of products that enhance daily life.

Celebratory Campaigns: Leveraging holidays, festivals, and special occasions to promote products can trigger positive emotions. For example, chocolate brands often market their products as essential for celebrations and gifting.

2: Nostalgia:

Childhood Memories: Many FMCG brands evoke nostalgia by reminding consumers of their childhood or significant life moments. This emotional connection can foster brand loyalty.

Retro Packaging: Using vintage packaging designs can trigger fond memories and differentiate products on the shelf.

3: Comfort and Security:

Reliability and Trust: Products that emphasize safety, reliability, and quality can evoke feelings of comfort and security. This is particularly important for categories like baby products, food, and personal care items.

Family Values: Marketing that focuses on family and home life can create a sense of warmth and trustworthiness, appealing to consumers' desire for stability and care.

4: Excitement and Adventure:

Innovation and Novelty: Introducing new and innovative products can generate excitement and appeal to consumers' sense of adventure and curiosity.

Experiential Marketing: Creating interactive and engaging experiences, such as in-store demonstrations and sampling, can trigger excitement and encourage trial purchases.

5: Guilt and Responsibility:

Health and Wellness: Highlighting the health benefits of products can appeal to consumers' desire to make responsible choices for themselves and their families.

Environmental Concerns: Promoting eco-friendly products and sustainable practices can resonate with consumers who feel a responsibility towards the environment.

6: Fear and Anxiety:

Problem-Solution Marketing: Addressing common concerns and problems, such as hygiene and health issues, can evoke a sense of urgency and prompt immediate action. For instance, hand sanitizers and disinfectants often use fear-based appeals to emphasize the importance of their products.

7: Social Connection and Belonging:

Community and Togetherness: Marketing that emphasizes social connections and belonging can foster a sense of community. Campaigns that show people coming together over a meal or sharing experiences can be particularly effective.

User-Generated Content: Encouraging consumers to share their experiences with a product on social media can create a sense of belonging and community around the brand.

Emotional Branding Strategies

1: Storytelling:

Brand Narratives: Creating a compelling brand story that resonates with consumers on an emotional level can foster deep connections. This could include the brand's history, mission, and values.

Customer Stories: Sharing real-life stories from customers who have had positive experiences with the product can add authenticity and relatability to the brand narrative.

2: Visual and Sensory Appeal:

Aesthetic Design: Using appealing visuals, colors, and designs that evoke specific emotions can enhance the emotional impact of packaging and advertising.

Sensory Marketing: Incorporating sensory elements such as appealing scents, textures, and sounds in the product and its packaging can create memorable experiences and emotional connections.

3: Cause-Related Marketing:

Social Responsibility: Aligning the brand with social causes and philanthropic efforts can evoke positive emotions and build a loyal customer base that shares the same values.

Environmental Initiatives: Promoting eco-friendly practices and products can appeal to consumers' environmental consciousness and create a positive brand image.

4: Personalization:

Customized Products: Offering personalized products or packaging can make consumers feel special and valued, enhancing their emotional connection to the brand.

Tailored Marketing: Using data and insights to create personalized marketing messages that resonate with individual consumers' preferences and emotions can increase engagement and loyalty.

5: Emotional Advertising:

Evocative Campaigns: Creating advertisements that tell a story, evoke emotions, and create a memorable experience can significantly impact consumer perceptions and behavior.

Music and Sound: The strategic use of music and sound in advertising can enhance the emotional appeal and make the message more memorable.

6: Interactive Engagement:

Social Media Campaigns: Engaging consumers through interactive social media campaigns, contests, and challenges can create excitement and a sense of community.

Experiential Marketing: Hosting events, pop-up stores, and interactive experiences that allow consumers to engage with the brand in a meaningful way can strengthen emotional connections.

7: Loyalty Programs:

Rewarding Loyalty: Implementing loyalty programs that reward repeat purchases and long-term commitment can make consumers feel appreciated and emotionally connected to the brand.

Exclusive Benefits: Offering exclusive benefits, such as early access to new products or special discounts, can enhance the sense of belonging and loyalty among consumers.

8: Transparency and Authenticity:

Honest Communication: Being transparent about product ingredients, sourcing, and manufacturing processes can build trust and credibility, fostering an emotional connection based on authenticity.

Brand Integrity: Maintaining consistent brand values and integrity in all marketing efforts can enhance the emotional bond with consumers who share those values.

Conclusion

Emotional triggers and branding strategies are powerful tools in the FMCG sector. By understanding and leveraging the emotional aspects of consumer behavior, brands can create deeper connections with their customers, foster loyalty, and drive purchasing decisions. The key is to craft marketing messages and experiences that resonate emotionally, whether through storytelling, visual appeal, personalization, or cause-related marketing.

In an increasingly competitive market, the ability to connect with consumers on an emotional level can be a significant differentiator, leading to sustained brand success and consumer loyalty.

Chapter 16
The Role of Advertising

Advertising is a critical component of marketing strategies in the FMCG sector. It shapes consumer perceptions, drives awareness, and influences purchasing decisions. This chapter explores the psychological principles underlying effective advertising and outlines successful advertising strategies specific to FMCG.

Psychological Principles in Advertising

1: Attention and Perception:

Visual Appeal: Attractive visuals, vibrant colors, and engaging imagery capture attention. Using high-quality graphics and appealing designs helps in making the advertisement stand out.

Motion and Animation: Incorporating motion and animation in digital ads can draw attention and make the message more engaging.

Contrast and Focus: Using contrast effectively (e.g., light vs. dark, big vs. small) and focusing on key elements guides viewers' attention to the most important parts of the ad.

2: Memory and Recall:

Repetition: Repeated exposure to an advertisement enhances recall and brand recognition. Consistent messaging across various platforms reinforces the brand.

Simplicity: Simple, clear, and concise messages are easier to remember. Avoiding clutter ensures that the key message is retained by the audience.

Jingles and Slogans: Catchy jingles and memorable slogans stick in consumers' minds, making it easier for them to recall the brand and its message.

3: Emotional Engagement:

Emotional Appeals: Ads that evoke emotions such as happiness, nostalgia, love, or excitement create a stronger connection with consumers. Emotional engagement enhances brand loyalty and recall.

Storytelling: Narratives and stories resonate more with audiences than straightforward facts. Creating a relatable story around the product or brand can deepen emotional ties.

4: Social Proof and Influence:

Testimonials and Reviews: Featuring customer testimonials and reviews builds credibility and trust. Consumers are influenced by the experiences of others.

Celebrity Endorsements: Celebrities and influencers can sway consumer opinions and enhance the perceived value of a product through their endorsements.

5: Persuasion Techniques:

Scarcity and Urgency: Highlighting limited availability or time-sensitive offers creates a sense of urgency, prompting immediate action.

Authority: Using experts or authoritative figures to endorse a product can enhance credibility and persuasiveness.

Consistency and Commitment: Encouraging small commitments (like signing up for a newsletter) can lead to larger commitments (like purchasing a product) due to the principle of consistency.

6: Cognitive Ease:

Fluency: Messages that are easy to process and understand are more likely to be persuasive. Using simple language, clear fonts, and straightforward layouts enhances cognitive ease.

Familiarity: Familiar faces, themes, or settings in ads create a sense of comfort and trust, making consumers more receptive to the message.

Effective Advertising Strategies in FMCG

1: Multi-Channel Campaigns:

Integrated Marketing: Combining TV, radio, print, online, and social media advertising ensures wide reach and reinforces the message across different touchpoints.

Consistent Messaging: Maintaining a consistent message across all channels strengthens brand identity and ensures that the core message is effectively communicated.

2: Targeted Advertising:

Demographic Segmentation: Tailoring ads to specific demographic groups (age, gender, income) ensures relevance and effectiveness.

Behavioral Targeting: Using data on consumer behavior (browsing history, purchase patterns) to deliver personalized ads that align with individual preferences and needs.

3: Content Marketing:

Educational Content: Creating informative and valuable content that addresses consumer needs and questions builds trust and positions the brand as an expert in the field.

Engaging Formats: Utilizing videos, infographics, blog posts, and social media updates to deliver content in engaging and easily digestible formats.

4: Emotional and Sensory Appeals:

Emotional Storytelling: Crafting stories that evoke emotions and connect with consumers on a personal level enhances brand affinity and recall.

Sensory Experiences: Using sensory elements (like appealing visuals, catchy sounds, and engaging narratives) to create memorable advertising experiences.

5: Interactive and Experiential Marketing:

Interactive Ads: Incorporating interactive elements such as quizzes, polls, and augmented reality experiences in digital ads increases engagement and involvement.

Experiential Campaigns: Hosting events, pop-up stores, and live demonstrations provide hands-on experiences that foster a deeper connection with the brand.

6: Social Media and Influencer Marketing:

Social Media Engagement: Leveraging platforms like Instagram, Facebook, Twitter, and TikTok to engage with consumers through posts, stories, and live sessions.

Influencer Collaborations: Partnering with influencers who align with the brand values to reach their followers and enhance credibility.

7: Seasonal and Event-Based Campaigns:

Festive Promotions: Aligning advertising campaigns with festivals, holidays, and significant events to capitalize on heightened consumer activity.

Event Sponsorships: Sponsoring popular events (like sports tournaments, cultural festivals) to increase visibility and association with positive experiences.

8: Test and Optimize:

A/B Testing: Continuously testing different versions of ads (headlines, images, calls to action) to determine what resonates best with the audience.

Performance Analytics: Using data analytics to monitor the performance of advertising campaigns and optimize strategies based on insights and feedback.

Case Studies: Successful FMCG Advertising Campaigns

1: Coca-Cola's "Share a Coke" Campaign:

Personalization: The campaign featured bottles with popular names, encouraging consumers to find and share bottles with their names or friends' names. This personalized approach created an emotional connection and boosted sales.

Social Media Engagement: The campaign leveraged social media platforms, encouraging consumers to share pictures with their personalized Coke bottles, further amplifying its reach and impact.

2: Dove's "Real Beauty" Campaign:

Emotional Appeal: Dove's campaign focused on celebrating natural beauty and challenging conventional beauty standards. This emotional and empowering message resonated with a wide audience.

Authenticity: Featuring real women instead of models added authenticity and relatability, strengthening the emotional bond with consumers.

3: Old Spice's "The Man Your Man Could Smell Like" Campaign:

Humor and Wit: The humorous and witty ads featuring Isaiah Mustafa quickly went viral, capturing attention and creating a memorable brand image.

Multi-Channel Strategy: The campaign effectively used TV, online, and social media channels to maximize reach and engagement.

Conclusion

Effective advertising in the FMCG sector requires a deep understanding of psychological principles and strategic implementation across various channels. By leveraging attention-capturing techniques, emotional engagement, social proof, and persuasive messaging, FMCG brands can create impactful ads that resonate with consumers and drive purchasing decisions. Continuous optimization, personalized approaches, and a focus on creating memorable experiences are key to successful advertising in this competitive industry.

Chapter 17
Consumer Behavior in the Digital Age

The digital revolution has dramatically transformed consumer behavior, particularly in the FMCG sector. Online shopping has become a major force, and digital marketing strategies are now crucial for influencing FMCG purchases. This chapter explores the dynamics of online shopping behavior and the significant impact of digital marketing on consumer decisions.

Online Shopping Behavior

1: Convenience and Accessibility:

24/7 Availability: Online shopping allows consumers to shop at any time, providing unparalleled convenience. This is especially important for FMCG products, which are often needed urgently.

Ease of Use: User-friendly websites and mobile apps enhance the shopping experience, making it easier for consumers to browse, select, and purchase products.

2: Comparison Shopping:

Price Comparison: Consumers can easily compare prices across different online retailers, which influences their purchasing decisions. Price comparison tools and apps further facilitate this process.

Product Reviews and Ratings: Access to customer reviews and ratings helps consumers make informed decisions. Positive reviews can boost confidence in a product, while negative reviews can deter purchases.

3: Personalization and Recommendations:

Tailored Shopping Experience: Online retailers use algorithms to personalize the shopping experience, recommending products based on past purchases and browsing behavior. This increases the likelihood of impulse buys and repeat purchases.

Email and Push Notifications: Personalized email campaigns and app notifications keep consumers informed about promotions, new products, and personalized offers.

4: Mobile Commerce:

Growth of Mobile Shopping: The increasing use of smartphones has led to a rise in mobile commerce. Consumers appreciate the ability to shop on-the-go, which is facilitated by mobile-optimized websites and apps.

Mobile Payments: The availability of secure and convenient mobile payment options, such as digital wallets and one-click payments, enhances the appeal of online shopping.

5: Social Shopping:

Social Media Influence: Social media platforms play a significant role in influencing purchasing decisions. Recommendations from friends, influencers, and social media ads can drive sales.

Social Commerce Features: Features like shoppable posts and in-app purchases on platforms such as Instagram and Facebook streamline the buying process, making it easier for consumers to purchase directly from social media.

6: Subscription Services:

Convenience of Subscriptions: Subscription services for FMCG products, such as meal kits, beauty boxes, and household essentials, provide convenience and often include personalized product selections.

Automatic Renewals: Automatic subscription renewals ensure a steady supply of frequently used items, reducing the need for repeat purchasing decisions.

7: Customer Service and Support:

Live Chat and Chatbots: Immediate assistance through live chat and AI-powered chatbots enhances customer satisfaction and can address queries that might otherwise deter a purchase.

Easy Returns and Refunds: Clear and hassle-free return policies increase consumer confidence in online shopping, making them more likely to buy.

Influence of Digital Marketing on FMCG Purchases

1: Search Engine Optimization (SEO):

Visibility in Search Results: Effective SEO strategies ensure that FMCG products appear prominently in search engine results, increasing the likelihood of clicks and purchases.

Content Marketing: Creating valuable content, such as blog posts and how-to guides, can drive organic traffic to FMCG websites and enhance brand authority.

2: Pay-Per-Click (PPC) Advertising:

Targeted Ads: PPC campaigns allow brands to target specific demographics, interests, and behaviors, ensuring that ads reach the most relevant audiences.

Retargeting: Retargeting ads remind consumers of products they viewed but didn't purchase, encouraging them to return and complete the transaction.

3: Social Media Marketing:

Engaging Content: Creating engaging and shareable content on social media platforms increases brand visibility and fosters consumer engagement.

Influencer Collaborations: Partnering with influencers who align with the brand's values can amplify reach and impact, leveraging their followers to drive FMCG purchases.

4: Email Marketing:

Personalized Campaigns: Segmented email lists and personalized content ensure that messages are relevant to the recipients, increasing open rates and conversions.

Promotional Offers: Exclusive discounts, special offers, and limited-time promotions communicated via email can prompt immediate purchases.

5: Affiliate Marketing:

Partnerships with Affiliates: Collaborating with affiliate marketers who promote products through their blogs, websites, and social media channels can drive traffic and sales.

Performance-Based Commissions: Affiliates earn commissions based on sales generated, incentivizing them to effectively market FMCG products.

6: Content Marketing and Storytelling:

Educational Content: Providing informative and valuable content that addresses consumer needs and pain points can build trust and brand loyalty.

Brand Storytelling: Sharing the brand's story and values through various digital platforms creates an emotional connection with consumers.

7: Video Marketing:

Product Demonstrations: Videos showcasing product usage, benefits, and unboxing experiences can enhance understanding and appeal.

Live Streaming: Live streaming events, such as product launches and Q&A sessions, engage consumers in real-time and create a sense of urgency.

8: Influencer Marketing:

Authentic Endorsements: Influencers who genuinely use and endorse FMCG products can create authentic connections with their audience, driving trust and sales.

Sponsored Content: Sponsored posts and stories on social media platforms can effectively highlight product features and benefits.

9: User-Generated Content (UGC):

Consumer Reviews and Testimonials: Encouraging satisfied customers to share their experiences and reviews creates social proof and builds trust.

UGC Campaigns: Running campaigns that encourage consumers to share photos and videos of themselves using the products can enhance engagement and reach.

10: Data Analytics and Insights:

Consumer Behavior Analysis: Leveraging data analytics to understand consumer behavior, preferences, and trends enables brands to tailor their marketing strategies effectively.

Performance Metrics: Tracking key performance indicators (KPIs) such as click-through rates, conversion rates, and return on investment (ROI) helps optimize digital marketing efforts.

Case Studies: Successful Digital Marketing Campaigns

1: Procter & Gamble's (P&G) "Thank You, Mom" Campaign:

Emotional Storytelling: P&G's campaign highlighted the role of mothers in supporting Olympic athletes, creating an emotional connection with consumers.

Multi-Platform Strategy: The campaign used a combination of video ads, social media posts, and a dedicated microsite to reach a broad audience.

2: Unilever's Dove "Real Beauty Sketches":

Viral Video: Dove's campaign featured a video showcasing how women perceive their own beauty compared to how others see them, which went viral and sparked conversations about beauty standards.

Social Media Engagement: The campaign encouraged women to share their own stories on social media, amplifying its reach and impact.

3: Amazon's Prime Day:

Exclusive Offers: Amazon's annual Prime Day event offers exclusive discounts to Prime members, driving significant sales and increasing membership sign-ups.

Cross-Channel Promotion: The event is promoted through email marketing, social media, PPC ads, and on-site banners, ensuring maximum visibility.

Conclusion

The digital age has revolutionized consumer behavior, particularly in the FMCG sector. Online shopping behavior is influenced by convenience, personalization, social proof, and mobile accessibility. Digital marketing plays a crucial role in shaping purchasing decisions, with strategies such as SEO, PPC, social media marketing, and influencer collaborations proving highly effective. By understanding and leveraging these dynamics, FMCG brands can enhance their reach, engagement, and sales in the competitive digital marketplace.

Chapter 18
Consumer Satisfaction and Post-Purchase Behavior

Understanding consumer satisfaction and post-purchase behavior is crucial for the long-term success of FMCG brands. This chapter examines the factors that influence consumer satisfaction, explores the phenomenon of post-purchase dissonance, and discusses strategies for fostering loyalty among consumers.

Factors Influencing Satisfaction

1: Product Quality:

Performance: The product must meet or exceed consumer expectations in terms of performance. For FMCG products, this includes effectiveness, taste, durability, and overall usability.

Consistency: Consistency in product quality across different batches ensures that consumers have a reliable and predictable experience, fostering trust and satisfaction.

2: Value for Money:

Price-Quality Ratio: Consumers assess whether the quality of the product justifies its price. High perceived value, where quality meets or exceeds expectations for the price paid, enhances satisfaction.

Competitive Pricing: Offering competitive prices relative to similar products in the market can increase satisfaction by providing perceived value.

3: Packaging:

Functionality: Easy-to-use and convenient packaging can significantly enhance consumer satisfaction. For example, resealable bags or easy-pour containers add practical value.

Aesthetic Appeal: Attractive and visually appealing packaging can positively influence perceptions of the product and enhance satisfaction.

4: Brand Reputation:

Trust and Reliability: A strong brand reputation built on trust and reliability positively influences consumer satisfaction. Consumers are more likely to be satisfied with products from brands they trust.

Positive Associations: Brands that evoke positive emotions and associations through effective branding and marketing are more likely to satisfy consumers.

5: Customer Service:

Responsive Support: Access to responsive and helpful customer service enhances satisfaction. Efficient handling of inquiries, complaints, and returns contributes to a positive post-purchase experience.

Problem Resolution: Quick and fair resolution of any issues or defects with the product can mitigate dissatisfaction and reinforce consumer loyalty.

6: Product Availability:

Stock Consistency: Consistent availability of products ensures that consumers can repurchase their preferred items without inconvenience, contributing to ongoing satisfaction.

Distribution Channels: Wide availability across various distribution channels, both online and offline, increases consumer convenience and satisfaction.

7: User Experience:

Ease of Use: Products that are easy and intuitive to use increase satisfaction by minimizing effort and frustration.

Compatibility: For products that are part of a larger ecosystem (e.g., refills for a cleaning system), compatibility and seamless integration enhance satisfaction.

8: Post-Purchase Communication:

Follow-Up: Follow-up communication, such as thank-you emails or surveys, can enhance satisfaction by showing that the brand values consumer feedback and engagement.

Information and Tips: Providing information on how to best use the product or additional tips and tricks can improve the consumer experience and satisfaction.

Post-Purchase Dissonance and Loyalty

1: Post-Purchase Dissonance:

Definition: Post-purchase dissonance, also known as buyer's remorse, occurs when consumers experience doubt or anxiety after making a purchase. This is often due to perceived discrepancies between expectations and the actual product experience.

Causes: Common causes include high financial investment, conflicting information, and pressure to make a quick decision. For FMCG products, dissonance can arise if the product does not meet expectations or if there are negative reviews or feedback from others.

2: Mitigating Post-Purchase Dissonance:

Reassurance: Providing reassurance through follow-up communication can alleviate dissonance. This includes thank-you emails, satisfaction surveys, and usage tips.

Positive Reinforcement: Highlighting the benefits and positive aspects of the product in post-purchase communications can reinforce the consumer's decision.

Return and Exchange Policies: Clear and hassle-free return and exchange policies can reduce anxiety and provide a safety net for dissatisfied consumers.

Customer Support: Accessible and supportive customer service can address any concerns or issues, mitigating dissonance and improving overall satisfaction.

3: Building Loyalty:

Consistency and Reliability: Delivering consistent product quality and reliability builds trust and encourages repeat purchases. Consumers who can rely on a brand are more likely to remain loyal.

Loyalty Programs: Implementing loyalty programs that reward repeat purchases with discounts, exclusive offers, or points that can be redeemed for rewards fosters long-term loyalty.

Personalized Experience: Offering personalized experiences and tailored recommendations based on consumer preferences and purchase history can enhance loyalty.

Engagement and Community: Creating a sense of community through social media engagement, events, and interactive campaigns strengthens the emotional connection between consumers and the brand.

Positive Brand Experience: Ensuring that every interaction with the brand, from marketing to customer service, is positive and consistent reinforces loyalty.

4: Case Studies: Successful Strategies for Enhancing Satisfaction and Loyalty:

Apple's Customer Experience: Apple is renowned for its exceptional customer service and consistent product quality. Their Genius Bar provides personalized support, while their seamless integration of products enhances user satisfaction and loyalty.

Amazon Prime: Amazon's Prime membership program offers a range of benefits, including free shipping, exclusive deals, and access to streaming services. This comprehensive value proposition increases customer satisfaction and fosters loyalty.

Starbucks Rewards: Starbucks' loyalty program offers personalized rewards, free drinks, and exclusive offers, encouraging repeat visits and creating a strong emotional connection with customers.

Conclusion

Consumer satisfaction and post-purchase behavior are critical components of successful FMCG marketing. By understanding the factors that influence satisfaction, brands can enhance their products and services to meet consumer expectations. Addressing post-purchase dissonance through reassurance, support, and flexible policies can mitigate negative experiences and foster loyalty. Building long-term loyalty requires consistent quality, personalized experiences, and engaging consumer interactions. Through these strategies, FMCG brands can create lasting relationships with their customers, driving repeat purchases and sustained success in the marketplace.

Chapter 19
Ethical Considerations in Consumer Behavior

Ethical considerations are becoming increasingly important in consumer behavior, especially in the FMCG sector. Consumers are more aware of and concerned about the ethical implications of their purchases. This chapter delves into the trends in ethical consumerism and the role of corporate social responsibility (CSR) in the FMCG industry.

Ethical Consumerism Trends

1: Sustainable Consumption:

Environmental Impact: Consumers are increasingly considering the environmental impact of their purchases.

They prefer products that are eco-friendly, have sustainable packaging, and come from companies that minimize their carbon footprint.

Resource Efficiency: Products made using fewer resources and generating less waste are gaining popularity. Consumers are looking for brands that prioritize resource efficiency in their production processes.

2: Fair Trade and Labor Practices:

Fair Trade Certification: Products with fair trade certification ensure that producers, especially in developing countries, receive fair wages and work under good conditions. Consumers are more inclined to support brands that adhere to fair trade principles.

Ethical Labor Practices: Awareness of labor conditions in supply chains influences purchasing decisions. Brands that commit to ethical labor practices, such as prohibiting child labor and ensuring safe working environments, are favored by consumers.

3: Animal Welfare:

Cruelty-Free Products: Consumers are increasingly seeking out products that are not tested on animals. Cruelty-free certifications and labels help consumers make informed choices.

Vegan Products: The demand for vegan products, which do not contain any animal-derived ingredients, is on the rise. This trend reflects broader ethical considerations about animal rights and environmental sustainability.

4: Transparency and Traceability:

Supply Chain Transparency: Consumers want to know where their products come from and how they are made. Brands that provide detailed information about their supply chains and sourcing practices build trust and loyalty.

Ingredient Transparency: Clear labeling and disclosure of all ingredients used in products, particularly in food and personal care items, are important for consumers concerned about health and safety.

5: Social Impact:

Community Support: Brands that support local communities through initiatives like education, healthcare, and economic development resonate with consumers who value social impact.

Inclusive Practices: Inclusive business practices, such as diversity in hiring and promoting gender equality, positively influence consumer perceptions and purchasing decisions.

6: Ethical Marketing:

Honest Advertising: Ethical marketing involves truthful advertising that does not mislead consumers. Brands that are honest about their products' benefits and limitations earn consumer trust.

Avoiding Exploitation: Ethical marketing avoids exploiting sensitive issues or demographics for profit. It focuses on creating positive, respectful, and inclusive campaigns.

Corporate Social Responsibility in FMCG

1: Environmental Sustainability Initiatives:

Eco-Friendly Packaging: Many FMCG companies are adopting sustainable packaging solutions, such as biodegradable materials, recyclable packaging, and reducing plastic usage. This not only reduces environmental impact but also appeals to eco-conscious consumers.

Carbon Neutrality: Companies are committing to reducing their carbon footprints and achieving carbon neutrality. Initiatives include using renewable energy sources, offsetting emissions, and improving energy efficiency in manufacturing processes.

2: Sustainable Sourcing:

Ethical Supply Chains: Ensuring that raw materials are sourced ethically and sustainably is a key aspect of CSR. This includes sourcing from suppliers who adhere to fair labor practices and environmental standards.

Supporting Small Producers: Many FMCG companies support small-scale and local producers, particularly in developing countries, to promote fair trade and sustainable agricultural practices.

3: Social Equity and Community Development:

Community Engagement: FMCG companies engage in community development projects, such as building schools, providing clean water, and supporting healthcare initiatives. These efforts contribute to social equity and enhance brand reputation.

Employee Welfare: Ensuring fair wages, safe working conditions, and opportunities for career growth within the company demonstrates a commitment to employee welfare and social responsibility.

4: Health and Well-being:

Product Safety and Quality: Ensuring the safety and quality of products is a fundamental aspect of CSR. This includes rigorous testing, transparent labeling, and adhering to health and safety regulations.

Promoting Healthy Lifestyles: FMCG companies can promote healthy lifestyles through their product offerings, such as providing healthier food options, reducing sugar and salt content, and encouraging physical activity.

5: Ethical Business Practices:

Corporate Governance: Good corporate governance practices, such as transparency, accountability, and ethical decision-making, are essential for maintaining consumer trust and integrity.

Anti-Corruption Measures: Implementing anti-corruption measures and ensuring compliance with legal and ethical standards in all business operations are crucial aspects of ethical business practices.

6: Stakeholder Engagement:

Consumer Feedback: Actively seeking and responding to consumer feedback helps companies align their CSR initiatives with consumer expectations and improve their products and services.

Collaborations and Partnerships: Partnering with non-profits, government agencies, and other organizations to address social and environmental issues can amplify the impact of CSR efforts.

Case Studies: Successful CSR Initiatives in FMCG

1: Unilever's Sustainable Living Plan:

Comprehensive Approach: Unilever's Sustainable Living Plan focuses on improving health and well-being, reducing environmental impact, and enhancing livelihoods. Initiatives include sourcing 100% of agricultural raw materials sustainably and reducing greenhouse gas emissions.

Brand-Specific Initiatives: Unilever brands like Dove, Lifebuoy, and Knorr have specific initiatives aligned with the Sustainable Living Plan, such as promoting self-esteem, improving hygiene, and supporting sustainable agriculture.

2: Procter & Gamble's (P&G) Environmental Sustainability:

Ambitious Goals: P&G has set ambitious sustainability goals, including making 100% of its packaging recyclable or reusable by 2030 and achieving carbon neutrality for its operations.

Waste Reduction: P&G has implemented waste reduction strategies, such as reducing water usage in manufacturing processes and using renewable energy sources.

3: Nestlé's Creating Shared Value (CSV):

Holistic Approach: Nestlé's CSV approach focuses on nutrition, water, and rural development. Initiatives include improving access to clean water, enhancing food security, and supporting smallholder farmers.

Health and Nutrition: Nestlé has committed to reducing sugar, salt, and saturated fat in its products and increasing the availability of healthier food options.

Conclusion

Ethical consumerism and CSR are integral to the FMCG industry's future. As consumers become more aware of the ethical implications of their purchases, they increasingly favor brands that align with their values. FMCG companies that adopt sustainable, fair, and transparent practices not only enhance consumer satisfaction and loyalty but also contribute positively to society and the environment. By integrating ethical considerations into their business strategies, FMCG brands can build a sustainable and responsible future.

Chapter 20
Innovation and Consumer Adoption

Innovation is a driving force in the FMCG sector, influencing how consumers perceive, adopt, and interact with new products. This chapter explores the dynamics of adopting new products in the FMCG industry, examines the innovation strategies employed by companies, and delves into the psychological factors that influence consumer adoption.

Adopting New Products in FMCG

1: Understanding the Adoption Process:

Awareness: Consumers must first become aware of the new product. Effective marketing and advertising campaigns play a crucial role in this stage.

Interest: Once aware, consumers develop an interest in learning more about the product. This is where detailed information and benefits are highlighted.

Evaluation: Consumers evaluate whether the new product meets their needs and expectations. Comparisons with existing products and alternatives occur at this stage.

Trial: A key stage where consumers try the product on a small scale to determine its suitability. Free samples, discounts, or smaller product sizes can facilitate this trial phase.

Adoption: If satisfied, consumers decide to regularly use the product. Successful adoption often leads to brand loyalty and repeat purchases.

2: Factors Influencing Adoption:

Relative Advantage: The perceived superiority of the new product over existing alternatives significantly influences adoption. This can include better quality, additional features, or lower cost.

Compatibility: The degree to which the new product aligns with consumers' existing values, experiences, and needs affects adoption. Products that fit seamlessly into consumers' lifestyles are more likely to be adopted.

Complexity: The ease of understanding and using the new product impacts adoption. Products that are simple and intuitive to use are more readily adopted.

Trialability: The ability to try the product before committing to a full purchase reduces perceived risk and enhances adoption rates.

Observability: The visibility of the new product's benefits to others influences adoption. Products that deliver noticeable and demonstrable benefits are more likely to be adopted.

Innovation Strategies and Consumer Psychology

1: Consumer-Centric Innovation:

Understanding Consumer Needs: Successful innovation starts with a deep understanding of consumer needs and pain points. Companies conduct market research, focus groups, and surveys to gather insights.

User Experience Design: Designing products with a focus on the user experience ensures that innovations meet consumer expectations and enhance satisfaction. This includes ergonomic design, intuitive interfaces, and convenient features.

2: Open Innovation and Collaboration:

Collaborative Partnerships: Partnering with other companies, research institutions, and start-ups can drive innovation. These collaborations bring diverse perspectives and expertise, leading to more innovative solutions.

Crowdsourcing: Engaging consumers in the innovation process through crowdsourcing ideas and feedback can lead to product improvements and new product ideas that resonate with consumers.

3: Sustainable Innovation:

Eco-Friendly Products: Innovating with sustainability in mind appeals to environmentally conscious consumers. This includes using eco-friendly materials, reducing waste, and improving energy efficiency.

Circular Economy: Developing products that support a circular economy, where materials are reused and recycled, enhances brand reputation and meets consumer demand for sustainable options.

4: Technology-Driven Innovation:

Digital Transformation: Leveraging digital technologies to create innovative products and services can differentiate a brand. This includes smart packaging, IoT-enabled products, and personalized digital experiences.

Artificial Intelligence: Using AI to analyze consumer data and predict trends enables companies to innovate proactively. AI can also enhance product functionality, such as smart assistants in home appliances.

5: Incremental vs. Disruptive Innovation:

Incremental Innovation: Gradual improvements and enhancements to existing products can sustain consumer interest and loyalty. This approach focuses on refining and optimizing products based on consumer feedback.

Disruptive Innovation: Introducing entirely new products that transform the market and consumer behavior can create significant competitive advantages. This approach often involves higher risk but can lead to substantial rewards.

6: Psychological Factors in Consumer Adoption:

Perceived Risk: The level of risk perceived by consumers in adopting a new product affects their willingness to try it. Companies can mitigate this by offering guarantees, free trials, and clear information.

Social Influence: Social factors, such as peer recommendations and influencer endorsements, play a significant role in adoption. Positive reviews and word-of-mouth can accelerate the adoption process.

Emotional Appeal: Creating an emotional connection with consumers through storytelling, branding, and marketing can enhance adoption. Products that evoke positive emotions and resonate with personal values are more likely to be adopted.

Behavioral Economics: Understanding how consumers make decisions, including biases and heuristics, can inform innovation strategies. For example, anchoring, framing, and the endowment effect can influence how new products are perceived and adopted.

Case Studies: Successful Innovation in FMCG

1: Procter & Gamble's Tide Pods:

Convenience and Simplicity: Tide Pods revolutionized laundry by offering a simple, convenient, and mess-free solution. The product's ease of use and effectiveness quickly gained consumer acceptance.

Marketing Strategy: P&G's marketing emphasized the product's convenience and superior cleaning power, effectively addressing consumer pain points and highlighting the product's relative advantage.

2: Unilever's Dove Real Beauty Campaign:

Emotional Connection: The Dove Real Beauty campaign focused on promoting real beauty and self-esteem. This emotional appeal resonated with consumers and created a strong brand connection.

Consumer-Centric Approach: By addressing the social issue of unrealistic beauty standards, Dove positioned itself as a brand that understands and supports its consumers, fostering loyalty and trust.

3: Nestlé's Nespresso:

Premium Experience: Nespresso transformed the coffee market by offering a premium, convenient coffee experience at home. The product's quality and ease of use appealed to coffee enthusiasts.

Subscription Model: The Nespresso Club and subscription model enhanced consumer loyalty by providing personalized services, exclusive offers, and a sense of community.

Conclusion

Innovation is essential for staying competitive in the FMCG sector. Understanding the adoption process and the factors that influence consumer behavior can help companies design effective innovation strategies. By focusing on consumer needs, leveraging technology, and addressing psychological factors, FMCG brands can successfully introduce new products that resonate with consumers and drive adoption. Sustainable and consumer-centric innovation not only enhances brand reputation but also fosters long-term loyalty and market success.

Chapter 21
Environmental and Sustainability Issues

As environmental concerns become increasingly prominent, both consumers and companies in the FMCG sector are placing a greater emphasis on sustainability. This chapter explores the trends in green consumerism and outlines sustainable practices adopted by FMCG companies to address these environmental challenges.

Green Consumerism Trends

1: Rise of Eco-Conscious Consumers:

Awareness and Education: With growing awareness about environmental issues such as climate change, pollution, and resource depletion, consumers are more informed and concerned about the ecological impact of their purchases.

Demand for Transparency: Consumers are demanding greater transparency from companies about their environmental practices and the sustainability of their products. They seek detailed information about sourcing, production processes, and environmental impact.

2: Preference for Sustainable Products:

Eco-Friendly Materials: Consumers are increasingly opting for products made from sustainable materials, such as biodegradable, recyclable, and renewable resources. Products with minimal packaging or eco-friendly packaging also appeal to green consumers.

Organic and Natural Products: The demand for organic and natural products, which are perceived as healthier and less harmful to the environment, is on the rise. This includes food, personal care items, and household products.

3: Support for Ethical Brands:

Corporate Social Responsibility (CSR): Brands that demonstrate a strong commitment to CSR, including environmental stewardship and ethical practices, earn the trust and loyalty of eco-conscious consumers.

Third-Party Certifications: Certifications such as Fair Trade, USDA Organic, and Rainforest Alliance provide assurance to consumers about the ethical and sustainable practices of brands.

4: Minimalism and Zero-Waste Movements:

Minimalist Lifestyle: The minimalist movement, which advocates for reduced consumption and prioritizing quality over quantity, is gaining traction. Consumers are seeking durable, multipurpose products that generate less waste.

Zero-Waste Initiatives: Zero-waste lifestyles, which aim to minimize waste production and promote recycling and composting, are influencing consumer behavior. Brands offering refillable, reusable, or package-free products are well-received.

5: Local and Sustainable Sourcing:

Locally Produced Goods: Consumers are showing a preference for locally produced goods, which often have a lower carbon footprint due to reduced transportation distances. Supporting local economies also aligns with ethical consumerism values.

Sustainable Agriculture: Products sourced from sustainable agricultural practices, including organic farming and regenerative agriculture, are gaining popularity as consumers prioritize environmental sustainability.

Sustainable Practices in FMCG

1: Eco-Friendly Packaging:

Biodegradable and Compostable Materials: FMCG companies are increasingly using biodegradable and compostable materials for packaging to reduce environmental impact. This includes plant-based plastics, paper, and cardboard.

Reducing Plastic Use: Efforts to reduce plastic use include eliminating single-use plastics, using recycled plastic, and developing alternative packaging solutions. Brands are innovating with materials like glass, metal, and biodegradable plastics.

2: Sustainable Sourcing:

Ethical Supply Chains: Ensuring that raw materials are sourced ethically and sustainably is crucial. This involves working with suppliers who adhere to fair labor practices and environmental standards.

Sustainable Agriculture: Companies are promoting sustainable agriculture practices, such as organic farming, agroforestry, and regenerative agriculture, to ensure long-term environmental health and resource availability.

3: Energy Efficiency and Carbon Footprint Reduction:

Renewable Energy: FMCG companies are investing in renewable energy sources, such as solar, wind, and hydroelectric power, to reduce their carbon footprint and reliance on fossil fuels.

Energy-Efficient Operations: Implementing energy-efficient technologies and practices in manufacturing processes, distribution, and retail operations helps reduce overall energy consumption and emissions.

4: Waste Reduction and Circular Economy:

Zero-Waste Goals: Some FMCG companies are setting ambitious zero-waste goals, aiming to eliminate waste across their operations. This includes reducing, reusing, and recycling materials wherever possible.

Circular Economy Practices: Embracing circular economy principles involves designing products and packaging for longevity, recyclability, and reuse. This reduces waste and maximizes resource efficiency.

5: Water Conservation:

Efficient Water Use: Implementing water-efficient practices in manufacturing processes, such as recycling water and using water-saving technologies, helps conserve this vital resource.

Protecting Water Sources: FMCG companies are also working to protect and restore water sources, ensuring sustainable water management in their supply chains and local communities.

6: Sustainable Product Development:

Eco-Innovation: Developing new products with sustainability at the forefront, such as using renewable materials, reducing environmental impact, and enhancing product lifespan, is a key focus for FMCG companies.

Lifecycle Analysis: Conducting lifecycle analyses to assess the environmental impact of products from raw material extraction to disposal helps identify opportunities for improvement and innovation.

Case Studies: Sustainable Practices in FMCG

1: Unilever's Sustainable Living Plan:

Comprehensive Sustainability Goals: Unilever's Sustainable Living Plan focuses on improving health and well-being, reducing environmental impact, and enhancing livelihoods. The company aims to halve the environmental footprint of its products by 2030.

Sustainable Sourcing: Unilever sources 100% of its agricultural raw materials sustainably and promotes sustainable agriculture practices among its suppliers.

2: Procter & Gamble's (P&G) Environmental Sustainability Efforts:

Ambitious Sustainability Goals: P&G has set goals to achieve 100% recyclable or reusable packaging by 2030 and to reduce greenhouse gas emissions by 50% across its operations.

Water Stewardship: P&G focuses on water conservation and efficiency, aiming to improve water management practices across its supply chains and communities where it operates.

3: Nestlé's Commitment to Sustainability:

Creating Shared Value (CSV): Nestlé's CSV approach prioritizes nutrition, water, and rural development. The company is committed to reducing its environmental footprint and promoting sustainable practices.

Plastic Waste Reduction: Nestlé is working towards making 100% of its packaging recyclable or reusable by 2025 and is actively reducing its use of virgin plastics.

Conclusion

Environmental and sustainability issues are at the forefront of consumer concerns and business strategies in the FMCG sector. Green consumerism trends highlight the growing demand for eco-friendly, ethical, and sustainable products. FMCG companies are responding by adopting a wide range of sustainable practices, from eco-friendly packaging and sustainable sourcing to energy efficiency and waste reduction. By prioritizing sustainability, these companies not only meet consumer expectations but also contribute to a healthier planet and a more sustainable future. Embracing sustainability is not just an ethical imperative but also a strategic advantage in the competitive FMCG market.

Chapter 22
Psychological Aspects of Brand Switching

Brand switching, the act of consumers changing from one brand to another, is a critical concept in the FMCG sector. Understanding the psychological aspects of brand switching helps companies develop strategies to retain customers and maintain loyalty in highly competitive markets. This chapter explores the reasons behind brand switching and the tactics companies can use to retain their customers.

Reasons for Brand Switching

1: Perceived Quality and Satisfaction:

Dissatisfaction with Current Brand: If a consumer is dissatisfied with the performance, quality, or overall experience of their current brand, they are likely to switch to a competitor. Common dissatisfaction points include poor product quality, ineffective customer service, or negative experiences.

Inconsistent Quality: Inconsistent product quality can lead to frustration and drive consumers to seek more reliable alternatives. Consistency is key in maintaining consumer trust and loyalty.

2: Price Sensitivity:

Price Changes: Significant price increases in a preferred brand can lead to consumers switching to more affordable options. Conversely, promotional pricing or discounts from competitors can attract price-sensitive consumers.

Perceived Value: Consumers evaluate the value they receive for the price they pay. If they perceive that a competitor offers better value for money, they may switch brands.

3: Variety Seeking:

Desire for New Experiences: Some consumers have a natural tendency to seek variety and try new products. This behavior, known as variety seeking, can lead to brand switching even when they are satisfied with their current brand.

Product Innovation: Innovative products and new offerings from competitors can entice consumers to switch brands, especially if the new products offer unique benefits or features.

4: Social Influences:

Peer Recommendations: Recommendations from friends, family, or social networks can strongly influence brand switching. Positive word-of-mouth about a competitor's brand can encourage consumers to switch.

Social Norms and Trends: Social trends and norms, such as the popularity of eco-friendly or health-conscious products, can drive consumers to switch brands that align with these values.

5: Marketing and Advertising:

Effective Advertising: Persuasive and impactful advertising campaigns by competitors can attract consumers and lead to brand switching. Emotional appeals, celebrity endorsements, and memorable messaging play significant roles.

Promotional Offers: Special promotions, such as discounts, buy-one-get-one-free offers, or loyalty rewards, can incentivize consumers to try new brands.

6: Availability and Convenience:

Product Availability: If a consumer's preferred brand is out of stock or not readily available, they may switch to an available alternative. Ensuring consistent product availability is crucial in retaining customers.

Convenience: Brands that offer greater convenience, such as easier access, better packaging, or more user-friendly products, are more likely to attract and retain consumers.

Retaining Customers in Competitive Markets

1: Enhancing Product Quality:

Consistent Quality Control: Implementing stringent quality control measures ensures that products consistently meet consumer expectations, reducing the likelihood of dissatisfaction and brand switching.

Continuous Improvement: Regularly gathering consumer feedback and continuously improving products based on this feedback helps maintain high levels of satisfaction and loyalty.

2: Competitive Pricing Strategies:

Value-Based Pricing: Offering competitive prices while emphasizing the superior value and benefits of the product can attract and retain price-sensitive consumers.

Promotional Incentives: Regular promotions, discounts, and loyalty programs can reward existing customers and deter them from switching to competitors.

3: Building Strong Brand Relationships:

Customer Engagement: Engaging with customers through various channels, such as social media, email newsletters, and events, helps build a strong emotional connection and brand loyalty.

Personalization: Personalized marketing efforts, such as tailored recommendations and offers based on consumer preferences and purchase history, enhance the customer experience and foster loyalty.

4: Effective Communication:

Transparent Communication: Being transparent about product benefits, company values, and any changes in the product or brand helps build trust and credibility with consumers.

Responsive Customer Service: Providing excellent customer service and promptly addressing consumer concerns and feedback can prevent dissatisfaction and brand switching.

5: Innovation and Differentiation:

Product Innovation: Continuously innovating and introducing new products or features that meet evolving consumer needs and preferences keeps the brand relevant and competitive.

Unique Selling Proposition (USP): Clearly communicating the unique benefits and differentiators of the brand helps consumers understand why they should remain loyal.

6: Leveraging Social Proof:

Positive Reviews and Testimonials: Showcasing positive reviews, testimonials, and user-generated content on various platforms can influence potential switchers and reinforce brand loyalty.

Influencer Partnerships: Collaborating with influencers who align with the brand values and target audience can enhance credibility and attract new consumers while retaining existing ones.

7: Sustainability and Ethical Practices:

Sustainable Initiatives: Demonstrating a commitment to sustainability and ethical practices resonates with environmentally and socially conscious consumers, fostering loyalty.

Corporate Social Responsibility (CSR): Engaging in CSR activities and communicating these efforts to consumers helps build a positive brand image and loyalty.

Case Studies: Successful Customer Retention Strategies

1: Coca-Cola's Personalized Marketing:

Share a Coke Campaign: Coca-Cola's "Share a Coke" campaign, which featured personalized names on bottles, created a personal connection with consumers and encouraged brand loyalty through emotional engagement.

Consistent Quality and Availability: Coca-Cola ensures consistent product quality and widespread availability, making it a reliable choice for consumers.

2: Apple's Customer-Centric Approach:

Exceptional Customer Service: Apple's focus on providing exceptional customer service through its Genius Bar and support channels helps build strong brand loyalty.

Innovative Products: Continuous innovation and the introduction of new products, such as the iPhone and iPad, keep consumers engaged and loyal to the brand.

3: Procter & Gamble's Tide Loyalty Programs:

Rewards and Incentives: P&G's Tide brand uses loyalty programs, such as rewards points for purchases and exclusive offers for loyal customers, to retain consumers.

Consistent Quality and Innovation: Tide's commitment to consistent quality and innovation, such as Tide Pods, keeps consumers satisfied and loyal.

Conclusion

Understanding the psychological aspects of brand switching is crucial for FMCG companies aiming to retain customers in competitive markets. By addressing the reasons behind brand switching, such as dissatisfaction, price sensitivity, and desire for variety, companies can develop effective strategies to retain customers. Enhancing product quality, competitive pricing, strong brand relationships, effective communication, innovation, leveraging social proof, and sustainability initiatives are key to building and maintaining customer loyalty. In the dynamic FMCG landscape, retaining customers through these strategies not only ensures sustained business success but also fosters long-term brand loyalty and trust.

Chapter 23
Consumer Behavior Research Methods

Understanding consumer behavior is essential for FMCG companies to develop effective marketing strategies and meet consumer needs. This chapter explores the various research methods used to study consumer behavior, including both qualitative and quantitative approaches. It also presents case studies that highlight the application of these methods in the FMCG sector.

Qualitative and Quantitative Approaches

1: Qualitative Research Methods:

In-Depth Interviews:

Description: One-on-one interviews that explore consumers' attitudes, motivations, and behaviors in detail. These interviews provide rich, nuanced insights into consumer experiences and preferences.

Application: Used to understand complex decision-making processes, emotional drivers, and personal experiences with products.

Focus Groups:

Description: Small, diverse groups of consumers discuss products, brands, or marketing strategies in a moderated setting. The interaction among participants can reveal group dynamics and collective perceptions.

Application: Useful for exploring consumer reactions to new product ideas, packaging designs, and advertising concepts.

Ethnographic Studies:

Description: Observational research where researchers immerse themselves in consumers' environments to understand their natural behaviors and interactions with products.

Application: Provides deep insights into how products are used in real-life contexts, identifying unmet needs and opportunities for innovation.

Projective Techniques:

Description: Indirect methods, such as word association, storytelling, or picture interpretation, used to uncover underlying motivations and attitudes that consumers may be unwilling or unable to articulate directly.

Application: Helps to reveal subconscious feelings and thoughts about brands and products.

2: Quantitative Research Methods:

Surveys and Questionnaires:

Description: Structured tools that collect data from a large sample of consumers, often using standardized questions. Surveys can be administered online, by phone, or in person.

Application: Useful for gathering statistically significant data on consumer preferences, satisfaction, and demographic characteristics.

Experiments:

Description: Controlled studies that manipulate one or more variables to observe their effect on consumer behavior. Experiments can be conducted in laboratories or in field settings.

Application: Ideal for testing hypotheses about cause-and-effect relationships, such as the impact of price changes on purchase intentions.

Observation:

Description: Systematic recording of consumer behavior in natural or simulated environments without direct interaction. This method captures actual behavior rather than self-reported data.

Application: Used to study in-store behavior, product usage patterns, and customer interactions with retail environments.

Data Analytics:

Description: Analysis of large datasets, often derived from digital sources like social media, e-commerce transactions, and customer databases. Techniques include statistical analysis, machine learning, and data mining.

Application: Helps identify trends, predict future behavior, and segment consumers based on their purchasing patterns and preferences.

Case Studies in FMCG Consumer Research

1: Case Study 1: Understanding Snack Preferences

Objective: A leading snack company aimed to understand the evolving preferences of millennial consumers.

Methodology:

Qualitative: Conducted focus groups with millennials to explore their snacking habits, motivations, and perceptions of health and convenience.

Quantitative: Distributed online surveys to a broader sample to quantify the findings from the focus groups.

Findings:

Millennials preferred snacks that were both healthy and convenient.

They valued transparent labeling and were influenced by social media endorsements.

Outcome: The company launched a new line of healthy snacks with clear, transparent packaging and partnered with social media influencers for promotion.

2: Case Study 2: Testing a New Beverage Concept

Objective: A beverage company wanted to test the market potential of a new flavored water product.

Methodology:

Quantitative: Conducted an online survey with a large sample to measure initial interest and purchase intent.

Qualitative: Followed up with in-depth interviews to understand the reasons behind consumers' interest or disinterest.

Findings:

The survey indicated a high level of interest, particularly among health-conscious consumers.

Interviews revealed that the natural ingredients and unique flavors were key drivers of interest.

Outcome: The company proceeded with a limited market launch, using the insights to refine their marketing messages and target health-conscious segments effectively.

3: Case Study 3: Enhancing In-Store Experience

Objective: A supermarket chain sought to improve the in-store shopping experience to increase customer satisfaction and loyalty.

Methodology:

Observation: Conducted in-store observations to identify pain points and areas for improvement in the shopping journey.

Surveys: Administered exit surveys to gather feedback on specific aspects of the shopping experience.

Findings:

Observations highlighted issues with store layout and signage that confused customers.

Surveys revealed that customers valued quick checkout processes and helpful staff.

Outcome: The supermarket chain reorganized store layouts, improved signage, and trained staff to be more customer-centric, resulting in higher satisfaction scores and repeat visits.

4: Case Study 4: Gauging Impact of a Social Media Campaign

Objective: An FMCG brand wanted to measure the effectiveness of a recent social media marketing campaign aimed at promoting a new product.

Methodology:

Data Analytics: Analyzed social media metrics, including engagement rates, shares, comments, and sentiment analysis.

Surveys: Conducted pre- and post-campaign surveys to measure changes in brand awareness and purchase intent.

Findings:

The campaign significantly increased engagement and positive sentiment on social media.

Surveys indicated a notable rise in brand awareness and a moderate increase in purchase intent among target demographics.

Outcome: The brand adjusted future campaigns to focus on content types and platforms that yielded the highest engagement and continued to monitor social media analytics for ongoing optimization.

Conclusion

Researching consumer behavior is essential for FMCG companies to develop effective strategies and meet consumer needs. Combining qualitative methods like in-depth interviews, focus groups, ethnographic studies, and projective techniques with quantitative methods like surveys, experiments, observation, and data analytics provides a comprehensive understanding of consumer behavior. These methods offer valuable insights that can drive product innovation, improve marketing strategies, and enhance customer experiences. By applying these research techniques, FMCG companies can stay ahead of market trends, anticipate consumer needs, and build stronger, more loyal customer relationships.

Chapter 24
Future Trends in Consumer Behavior

The landscape of consumer behavior is constantly evolving, influenced by technological advancements, changing societal values, and economic shifts. Understanding these future trends is crucial for FMCG companies to stay ahead of the curve and effectively cater to emerging consumer needs. This chapter explores how to predict consumer behavior shifts and identifies key emerging trends in FMCG marketing.

Predicting Consumer Behavior Shifts

1: Data Analytics and Predictive Modeling:

Big Data: Utilizing big data analytics allows companies to analyze vast amounts of data from various sources, such as social media, purchase history, and online behavior, to identify patterns and predict future behavior.

Machine Learning Algorithms: Machine learning models can analyze historical data to forecast future trends. These algorithms learn from data inputs and improve their accuracy over time, providing valuable predictions about consumer preferences and purchasing habits.

Customer Segmentation: Advanced segmentation techniques help identify distinct consumer groups with specific characteristics and predict how these segments might behave in the future. This allows for targeted marketing strategies.

2: Trend Analysis:

Social Media Monitoring: Analyzing conversations and trends on social media platforms provides real-time insights into emerging consumer interests and sentiments. Tools like sentiment analysis can gauge public opinion about brands and products.

Industry Reports and Market Research: Regularly reviewing industry reports, market research studies, and consumer surveys helps identify broader market trends and shifts in consumer behavior.

3: Scenario Planning:

Developing Scenarios: Creating various future scenarios based on different variables (e.g., economic conditions, technological advancements) helps companies anticipate potential changes in consumer behavior and prepare for multiple outcomes.

Stress Testing Strategies: Testing marketing and business strategies against these scenarios ensures that companies are resilient and adaptable to future changes.

4: Consumer Feedback and Insights:

Continuous Feedback Loops: Establishing continuous feedback mechanisms, such as customer reviews, surveys, and focus groups, allows companies to stay in tune with consumer needs and preferences.

Co-Creation with Consumers: Engaging consumers in the product development process through co-creation initiatives provides direct insights into their preferences and fosters brand loyalty.

Emerging Trends in FMCG Marketing

1: Personalization and Customization:

Tailored Experiences: Consumers increasingly expect personalized experiences. FMCG companies are using data to offer customized product recommendations, personalized marketing messages, and tailored promotions.

Custom Products: The demand for customizable products, such as personalized skincare routines or bespoke snack packs, is growing. Brands that offer customization options can better meet individual consumer needs.

2: Sustainability and Ethical Consumption:

Eco-Friendly Products: The trend towards sustainability continues to grow, with consumers seeking eco-friendly products and packaging. Brands are focusing on reducing their environmental footprint and communicating their sustainability efforts.

Ethical Sourcing: Ethical consumerism, which includes fair trade, cruelty-free, and socially responsible products, is becoming more important. Transparency in sourcing and ethical practices enhances brand trust.

3: Health and Wellness:

Health-Conscious Choices: The focus on health and wellness is driving demand for products with clean labels, natural ingredients, and health benefits. Functional foods and beverages, such as those with added vitamins or probiotics, are gaining popularity.

Mental Well-Being: Products promoting mental well-being, such as stress-relief snacks or mood-enhancing beverages, are emerging as consumers become more aware of mental health.

4: Digital and E-Commerce Growth:

Online Shopping: The shift towards online shopping continues to accelerate. FMCG brands are enhancing their e-commerce capabilities, optimizing online shopping experiences, and leveraging digital marketing to reach consumers.

Direct-to-Consumer (DTC) Models: Many brands are adopting DTC models, selling directly to consumers via their own online platforms. This approach allows for better control over the customer experience and direct access to consumer data.

5: Technology and Innovation:

Smart Packaging: Innovations in packaging, such as QR codes and NFC tags, provide consumers with additional product information, interactive experiences, and connectivity to digital platforms.

Augmented Reality (AR) and Virtual Reality (VR): AR and VR technologies are being used to create immersive shopping experiences, such as virtual try-ons or interactive product demos.

6: Convenience and On-Demand Solutions:

Quick and Easy Solutions: Time-strapped consumers are looking for convenient, on-the-go products. Ready-to-eat meals, single-serve portions, and easy-to-use products are becoming more popular.

Subscription Services: Subscription models for FMCG products, such as monthly snack boxes or beauty kits, provide convenience and encourage brand loyalty.

7: Community and Social Engagement:

Brand Communities: Building online and offline brand communities fosters a sense of belonging and loyalty among consumers. Brands are leveraging social media, forums, and events to engage with their communities.

Cause Marketing: Aligning with social causes and demonstrating corporate social responsibility resonates with consumers who prioritize brands that contribute to societal well-being.

Case Studies: Adapting to Future Trends

1: Procter & Gamble's Sustainability Initiatives:

Sustainable Packaging: P&G has committed to making 100% of its packaging recyclable or reusable by 2030. The company has introduced innovative packaging solutions, such as reusable aluminum bottles for its beauty brands.

Eco-Friendly Products: P&G's Tide brand offers eco-friendly laundry detergents with plant-based ingredients and reduced plastic packaging, catering to environmentally conscious consumers.

2: Unilever's Health and Wellness Focus:

Healthy Product Lines: Unilever has expanded its portfolio with health-focused products, such as the acquisition of the natural supplement brand Olly. The company is also reducing sugar, salt, and calories in its existing products.

Mental Health Campaigns: Unilever's Dove brand has launched campaigns promoting self-esteem and mental well-being, aligning with the growing consumer focus on mental health.

3: Nestlé's Digital Transformation:

E-Commerce Expansion: Nestlé has significantly expanded its e-commerce presence, optimizing online platforms and partnering with major e-retailers to reach more consumers.

Personalized Nutrition: Nestlé's personalized nutrition service, Persona, offers tailored vitamin packs based on individual health assessments, catering to the demand for customization and health-conscious products.

Conclusion

The future of consumer behavior in the FMCG sector is shaped by a multitude of factors, including technological advancements, shifting societal values, and economic trends. By leveraging data analytics, predictive modeling, and continuous consumer insights, companies can anticipate and adapt to these changes. Emerging trends such as personalization, sustainability, health and wellness, digital growth, technology innovation, convenience, and community engagement will define the future of FMCG marketing. FMCG companies that embrace these trends and remain agile in their strategies will be well-positioned to meet the evolving needs of consumers and maintain a competitive edge in the market.

Chapter 25
Conclusion

The study of consumer behavior is essential for understanding the complex dynamics that drive purchasing decisions in the FMCG sector. Throughout this book, we have explored the myriad factors influencing consumer behavior, from psychological and social influences to the impact of marketing strategies and emerging trends. In this final chapter, we summarize the key insights gleaned from these discussions and explore their implications for FMCG marketers aiming to thrive in an ever-evolving marketplace.

Summarizing Key Insights

1: Understanding Consumer Behavior in FMCG:

Consumers in the FMCG sector exhibit unique purchasing behaviors driven by convenience, price sensitivity, brand loyalty, and impulsive buying tendencies.

The study of consumer behavior in FMCG is crucial for tailoring marketing strategies to meet the specific needs and preferences of consumers in this fast-paced industry.

2: Consumer Decision-Making Process:

The decision-making process involves need recognition, information search, evaluation of alternatives, purchase decision, and post-purchase behavior.

Marketers must address each stage of this process to influence consumer choices effectively.

3: Psychological Factors:

Motivation, needs, perception, and sensation play significant roles in shaping consumer behavior.

Understanding these psychological factors helps marketers create compelling messages and product experiences that resonate with consumers.

4: Social and Cultural Influences:

Family, reference groups, social classes, culture, and subcultures profoundly impact consumer behavior.

Marketers must consider these social and cultural contexts to develop relevant and appealing marketing strategies.

5: Attitudes and Attitude Change:

Attitudes towards products and brands are formed through experiences and can be changed through effective marketing communications.

Strategies to change consumer attitudes include persuasive advertising, positive brand experiences, and endorsements.

6: Personality and Lifestyle:

Personality traits and lifestyles influence consumer preferences and purchasing behavior.

Brands that align with consumers' personalities and lifestyles can create stronger emotional connections and loyalty.

7: Perceived Quality and Brand Loyalty:

Perceived product quality is critical in determining consumer satisfaction and loyalty.

Building and maintaining high perceived quality and strong brand loyalty are essential for long-term success.

8: Pricing and Promotions:

Price perception and sensitivity affect purchasing decisions, and psychological pricing strategies can influence consumer behavior.

Promotions, discounts, and loyalty programs are effective in attracting and retaining customers.

9: Packaging and Visual Appeal:

Packaging plays a vital role in attracting attention, conveying brand identity, and influencing purchase decisions.

Thoughtful packaging design can enhance perceived value and differentiate products on crowded shelves.

10: Decision Heuristics and Impulse Buying:

Consumers often use decision heuristics, or mental shortcuts, in their purchasing decisions.

Understanding these heuristics and designing marketing strategies to prompt impulse buying can boost sales.

11: Cross-Cultural Behavior and Global Marketing:

Cultural differences significantly impact FMCG consumption patterns.

Adapting marketing strategies to fit local cultures is crucial for global market success.

12: Emotions and Advertising:

Emotions play a powerful role in purchasing decisions, and emotional branding can create lasting consumer connections.

Effective advertising leverages psychological principles to evoke desired emotions and drive brand engagement.

13: Digital Consumer Behavior:

The rise of digital technologies has transformed consumer behavior, with more consumers shopping online and engaging with brands through digital channels.

Digital marketing, e-commerce, and social media strategies are essential for reaching and influencing today's consumers.

14: Consumer Satisfaction and Post-Purchase Behavior:

Consumer satisfaction is influenced by product performance, customer service, and overall brand experience.

Addressing post-purchase dissonance and fostering loyalty through positive post-purchase experiences are critical for retaining customers.

15: Ethical Considerations and Sustainability:

Ethical consumerism and sustainability are increasingly important to consumers.

Companies that demonstrate corporate social responsibility and adopt sustainable practices can build trust and loyalty.

16: Innovation and Consumer Adoption:

Innovation drives consumer interest and adoption of new products.

Understanding the factors that influence innovation adoption helps companies successfully introduce new products to the market.

17: Psychological Aspects of Brand Switching:

Brand switching is influenced by dissatisfaction, price sensitivity, variety seeking, social influences, and competitive marketing.

Strategies to retain customers include enhancing product quality, offering competitive pricing, and building strong brand relationships.

18: Research Methods in Consumer Behavior:

Both qualitative and quantitative research methods provide valuable insights into consumer behavior.

Case studies demonstrate the practical application of these methods in the FMCG sector.

19: Future Trends in Consumer Behavior:

Predicting consumer behavior shifts through data analytics, trend analysis, scenario planning, and continuous feedback is essential for staying ahead.

Emerging trends such as personalization, sustainability, health and wellness, digital growth, technology innovation, convenience, and community engagement will shape the future of FMCG marketing.

Implications for FMCG Marketers

1: Consumer-Centric Strategies:

FMCG marketers must place consumers at the center of their strategies, understanding their needs, preferences, and behaviors to create relevant and appealing products and experiences.

2: Leveraging Data and Technology:

Utilizing data analytics and digital technologies allows for more precise targeting, personalized marketing, and efficient decision-making.

Investing in digital capabilities and staying abreast of technological advancements is crucial for competitive advantage.

3: Building Emotional Connections:

Emotional branding and storytelling can create deeper connections with consumers, fostering loyalty and advocacy.

Marketers should focus on creating memorable and emotionally resonant brand experiences.

4: Sustainability and Ethics:

Emphasizing sustainability and ethical practices aligns with consumer values and builds long-term trust and loyalty.

Transparency and authentic communication about sustainability efforts are essential.

5: Innovation and Adaptability:

Continual innovation in products, packaging, and marketing strategies is necessary to meet evolving consumer expectations.

Flexibility and adaptability in response to market changes and emerging trends ensure ongoing relevance.

6: Integrated Marketing Communication:

Coordinating marketing efforts across multiple channels, including traditional and digital media, ensures consistent messaging and maximizes reach.

An integrated approach enhances brand visibility and reinforces key messages.

7: Consumer Engagement and Community Building:

Engaging consumers through social media, events, and brand communities fosters a sense of belonging and loyalty.

Encouraging consumer participation and feedback helps build stronger relationships and enhances brand loyalty.

8: Focus on Health and Wellness:

Responding to the growing demand for health-conscious products with clean labels and functional benefits can capture a significant market segment.

Marketing efforts should highlight health benefits and align with consumers' wellness goals.

9: Convenience and On-Demand Services:

Offering convenient, on-the-go products and services meets the needs of busy consumers.

Subscription models and quick delivery options enhance convenience and drive repeat purchases.

10: Ethnographic and Cultural Sensitivity:

Understanding and respecting cultural differences in global markets is crucial for successful international marketing.

Tailoring products and marketing strategies to fit local cultures enhances relevance and acceptance.

Conclusion

The insights gained from studying consumer behavior are invaluable for FMCG marketers aiming to navigate the complexities of the modern marketplace. By understanding the psychological, social, and cultural factors that drive consumer behavior, marketers can develop effective strategies that resonate with consumers and foster long-term loyalty. Embracing emerging trends, leveraging data and technology, and maintaining a consumer-centric approach are key to staying competitive and achieving sustained success in the FMCG sector. As consumer behavior continues to evolve, staying informed and adaptable will ensure that FMCG brands remain relevant, trusted, and preferred by their target audiences.

If you like to read more interesting book some are the following!

www.ingramcontent.com/pod-product-compliance
Lightning Source LLC
Chambersburg PA
CBHW071919210526
45479CB00002B/477